D0875310

This first edition of *The Questions That Matter Most* has been graciously signed by the author.

"The entire time you are reading any novel, you are experiencing freedom and autonomy, and this is a political experience."

The Questions That Matter Most

JANE SMILEY

The Questions That Matter Most

READING, WRITING, AND THE EXERCISE OF FREEDOM

HEYDAY

Berkeley, California

Several of the essays in this book originally appeared, sometimes in slightly different form and with different titles, in the following publications: the *New Yorker*, *Fulbright Chronicles*, the anthology *The True Subject: Writers on Life and Craft* (Graywolf Press, 1993), the *Sydney Review of Books*, the anthology *Shakespeare's Sisters: Women Writers Bridge Five Centuries* (Folger Shakespeare Library, 2012), the *Los Angeles Times*, the anthology *March Sisters: On Life, Death, and Little Women* (Library of America, 2019), *Harper's*, *My Ántonia* by Willa Cather (100th anniversary edition, Vintage, 2018), the *Los Angeles Review of Books*, *Poison Penmanship* by Jessica Mitford (New York Review Books, 2010), the *Guardian*, and the *Atlantic*. "Reflections on St. Louis" is adapted from a talk given in 2020 at the St. Louis Botanical Garden for the Missouri Humanities Council.

Library of Congress Cataloging-in-Publication Data

Names: Smiley, Jane, author.
Title: The questions that matter most : reading, writing, and the exercise of freedom / Jane Smiley.
Description: Berkeley, California : Heyday, [2023]
Identifiers: LCCN 2022041766 | ISBN 9781597146050 (hardcover)
Subjects: LCSH: Smiley, Jane. | Smiley, Jane--Books and reading. | Novelists, American--20th century--Biography. | Novelists, American--21st century--Biography. | Authorship. | Fiction--History and criticism. | Fiction--Authorship. | LCGFT: Autobiographies. | Literary criticism. | Essays. | Short stories.
Classification: LCC PS3569.M39 Z46 2023 | DDC 813/.54 [B]--dc23/eng/20221122
LC record available at https://lccn.loc.gov/2022041766

Cover Photo: Elena Seibert
Cover Design: Frances Baca
Interior Design/Typesetting: *the*BookDesigners

Published by Heyday
P.O. Box 9145, Berkeley, California 94709
(510) 549-3564
heydaybooks.com

Printed in Chelsea, Michigan, by Sheridan Books, Inc.

10 9 8 7 6 5 4 3 2 1

Contents

Introduction

When I moved to California in 1996, I was following a horse. The horse's name was Terson (I called him Mr. T). I bought him from a stable in Wisconsin in 1993, and kept him in a barn outside Ames, Iowa, where I taught at Iowa State. But I was tired of nearly freezing to death when I rode him in the winter, and, by the way, my husband, Steve, who had grown up in Iowa, had spent some time in Santa Barbara and wanted to move back. Eventually, Steve and Mr. T. agreed on Carmel Valley, California. I could have said I was the native Californian, because I was born in LA, and my parents lived near Hollywood Park until I was about a year old, then moved back to the Midwest. Steve was born in Iowa, Mr. T in Germany. But no matter—like all migrants to California, we looked around and fell in love instantly with the new landscape and the ever-changing but (almost) always pleasant weather.

At the time, I was known for *A Thousand Acres* and *Moo*, one of them openly set in Iowa and the other one sort of set in Iowa, at a land grant university. The first thing I did (inspired by Mr. T) was decide that of course I could breed racehorses, and I did, though none of them were successful. But Mr. T and the horses I bred gave birth to *Horse Heaven*, and in order to understand racing and breeding, I took a wonderful tour of California— Del Mar, Santa Anita, Hollywood Park, Golden Gate Fields, Temecula, Coalinga, and Davis, with many stops in between (San Francisco, Los Angeles, Santa Barbara, San Diego). The first thing I learned about California was how beautiful it is; the second thing I learned was that the climate and the scenery change every time you turn a corner or go over a mountain. I experienced this just the other day when I was walking in Monterey, and I left the Del Monte Shopping Center for Don Dahvee Park. I saw a path that I had never taken before, and it took me straight into the woods along a creek, natural, chaotic, and messy, not half a mile from the designer handbags at Macy's.

•

Before I came to California, the only California writer I knew much about was John Steinbeck, from Salinas, who, judging by his works, was interested not only in the social world and the history of his native land but also in the landscape. In my favorite of his novels, *East of Eden*, he begins by describing the diversity of the Salinas Valley—the lupines and the poppies, the trees and the Spanish moss, the changing nature of the soil, and the danger and beauty of the Salinas River. All of his works take on economic and political themes too (obviously in *The Grapes of Wrath* and *Of Mice and Men*), but one of the things you can't help doing if you are a writer based in California is attempting to convey what it feels like to be here, moment by moment.

My family had one small connection to California—one of my grandfather's many older sisters ended up in Vallejo, married to an astronomer who was a true crackpot, and who was also from central Missouri. His name was Thomas Jefferson Jackson See, and he earned his stripes as a crackpot by ruthlessly opposing Einstein's theory of relativity until the day he died, convinced that the universe was made of ether. He worked for the US Navy, and was sent to Mare Island to use astronomy to tell the exact time of day and to let the captains of the ships know so that they could embark on their missions in the proper way. And so I went to Vallejo and Mare Island to look around, gathering the information I needed to write *Private Life* (published in 2010). I also discovered a blot on US, and California, history that I hadn't known about: the internment of the Japanese during World War II. (If you grew up in St. Louis, or elsewhere in Missouri, slavery and abolition and segregation were frequent topics of conversation.) What I learned about my great-aunt taught me more about the complicated history of California and more about the complicated history of my family.

•

When I began teaching creative writing at UC Riverside in 2015, I was pleased that my students were much more diverse than they had been in Iowa, and they all had stories to tell that were enlightening and dramatic. A term was ten weeks long, so every student had to produce a draft a week—three drafts each for the first three stories—and then to choose the story that most interested them and write a fourth draft of that one. Discussions of each draft lasted about twelve to fifteen minutes, and the students discussing each draft could not use words of judgment or praise—if they didn't like something, they had to ask a question, such as "Why does Mary disappear after the first three pages?" The result was that the students got more intrigued by the stories they were writing, and as they fixed things, the stories grew more complex and unique. Often, what the students who were reading the stories did not understand had to do with the connection between where the story was set and how this affected the main character and his or her friends and family. This meant that over time my students became more aware of the ecosystems and communities that they grew up in, and also more eager to depict them. Reading these stories worked for me, too, since there are so many enclaves in California that most of them are under the radar. Two examples of stories that my students were working on were one written by a female grad student about an insane asylum from the early twentieth century that was run by her ancestors, which explores the cruelty of the system, in part from the point of view of one of the women who works at the asylum; the other was by an male undergrad student, about a family escaping from Mexico after the father is killed by gang members—some members of the family have transportation, but some of them have to walk the whole way.

The books I assigned were meant to be an exploration for my students, but turned out to be an exploration for me, too. I was quite familiar with Sue Grafton and had been enjoying her mysteries since the late 1980s—in some sense she replaced my youthful obsession with Agatha Christie, and both my students and I enjoyed the way Grafton created suspense, but also how she portrayed the idiosyncratic locations in and around Santa Barbara. I was also familiar with *The Woman Warrior*, and I wanted my students to learn from the complexity of how the narrative mixes personal experience with traditional stories. We did not exactly read it as nonfiction, because the elements seemed imaginative to us and therefore worth learning from, for both fiction writers and nonfiction writers. In some sense, these books served my students as historical novels, about events and places that existed before they were born and that have now changed—I had felt the same pleasure in books I had read in school, such as *David Copperfield* and *Giants in the Earth*.

One book that my students and I found astonishingly compelling and informative was *Kindred*, by Octavia Butler, a novel that immerses modern readers in the experience of being enslaved in the mid-nineteenth century, and how that contrasts with the life the protagonist is leading in the present day. We understood that Butler was using science fiction to explore important issues that many of my students were familiar with but hadn't been asked to imagine in such detail before. *Little Scarlet*, by Walter Mosley, offered similar insights and feelings. Some of my students were from the LA area, and Mosley's dramatic depiction of the Watts riots and the racial issues surrounding them, plus the way he incorporated them into a thriller, was very alluring.

The more recent novels that we discussed showed them what they could aim for. I had spent a lot of time on an Ojibwa reservation in northern Wisconsin, but what Tommy Orange showed me and my students about the experiences of Native Americans in Oakland was completely new. The way that *There There* jumps around between the points of view of different characters (using first person, second person, and third person) also sparked discussions of the benefits that each point of view offers the reader and the author. I think that Orange, as the youngest of the authors, also provided my students a pathway to a fresh literary voice. I did not make them read *The Greenlanders*, but they had a similar experience when I assigned *The Good Men*, by Charmaine Craig, which was about religious conflicts in France in the fourteenth century, was a little shorter, and was written in a more accessible style than my novel. Many of my students were fascinated by events they had experienced or heard about, and *The Good Men* offered a way to talk about how to imagine those events in detail and put them on the page, even if, when you start, you have very little idea of how to understand them.

The book I assigned that I think my students and I appreciated the most was *The Sellout*, by Paul Beatty. I taught it in my comic novel class, and it was the perfect example of using a comic and satiric voice to lure the reader into seeing the absurdity of the world that the narrator is living in. It was a major prizewinner, but easy for my students, and for me, to relate to. It fit perfectly into the desire that I had for my students to feel the presence of the writers around them, busily working and depicting the places in California that my students knew and wanted to write about themselves.

•

What is my justification for collecting these essays? For me, it is that every novelist's life has taken place during times of turmoil, and many novelists choose to explore that turmoil (for example, Émile Zola). In this way, being a novelist becomes a form of education. Let's say that first comes fear, then comes rage, then comes curiosity, then comes a more complex curiosity as our imaginations encompass our characters and their feelings. One of the most controversial essays included here is a comparison of *Uncle Tom's Cabin* and *Huckleberry Finn*, titled "Say It Ain't So, Huck." I had read *Huckleberry Finn* in school and knew it was considered a great American novel, but

I had never read *Uncle Tom's Cabin* until I was forty-five and stuck in bed with a broken leg. *Uncle Tom's Cabin* is often derided, but when I read it, I thought it was much more complex and informative than *Huck Finn*, partly because Uncle Tom was not "an Uncle Tom"—he was a thoughtful and spiritual character—but mostly because the critics had overlooked Cassy, a determined and enterprising woman slave who manages to escape across the Ohio River with her child. I was incensed that a female author and her brave female character had to be denigrated while a male author who doesn't quite work out his plot gets to be number one. Before the age of the internet, my essay earned as much opprobrium as any essay ever printed in the *Atlantic*. What it did for me was make me consider the history of racism in the US in a way I'd never done before. I had been naive—I figured that if schools and public transit and our neighborhood were integrated, as they were when I was a child in St. Louis, racism must be behind us. Writing about those issues taught me how much further we had to go.

And then there was female exploitation and power, another aspect of *Uncle Tom's Cabin*. When I was a child, my mother worked at a newspaper, and then I went to a coed private school in St. Louis, and then I went to Vassar and the Iowa Writer's Workshop. There was never a moment when I suspected that being a girl and then a woman was somehow standing in my way. I wrote about what interested me; it got published. I was dedicated to doing what I wanted, and it never occurred to me to look at our junk house when I was in elementary school and compare it to the luxurious house a mile away that some relatives lived in. I didn't understand class or capitalism until I took up with a basketball-playing socialist in college. We lived in a small Marxist commune, had many discussions about exploitation and class, but never talked about feminism or art. Or race—there were no African Americans in our commune. By the time I started my writing career, I knew that even though the nuclear war I had feared as a child had never actually taken place, there were plenty of issues all around me to think about, learn about, and portray. As I wrote more novels and got interested in more subjects, I became more eager to explore those issues.

There was recently a short essay in the *Guardian* about how historical novels shouldn't exist. It was written by a man who had just published a historical novel, and I think he meant it as something of a spoof, but if I had been arguing the issue with him, I would have said that all novels are historical novels, because those that outlive their authors teach future readers what life was like from the authors' point of view at the time when the authors were writing them. A good example is Sir Walter Scott, one of the first novelists to explore eras several hundred years in the past (*Ivanhoe*, *Quentin Durward*). At the beginning of the nineteenth century, Scott did not have the archeological evidence we have, or other aspects of research that historians now employ, but he had the stories, passed down over generations, and he reimagined them and set them down in a new form—the novel, the historical novel. His work was hugely popular. The books are still readable and dramatic. My favorite of his are the novels he wrote about the religious conflicts of the seventeenth century, especially *The Tale of Old Mortality*. Is it accurate? As I was reading it, I was both enthralled and motivated to look up the history of those times and compare what historians had to say with what Scott wrote. And that is one thing historical novels do—they pull you in and make you wonder, not only about what really happened but also about how and why the author portrayed the events as he did. Because of this, I think that I often forgive and even thank authors of novels for truthfully representing the era they lived in. Yes, Anthony Trollope shows signs of antisemitism, and I don't like that, but it shows me who he is—he can't help but reveal it. It is also true of Trollope that he was more interested in, and more insightful about, the lives of his female characters than any nineteenth-century male writer that I can think of. Was that because his wife read his work, day by day, and gave him advice? I suspect it is. Novels and novelists are complex, and that is why I prefer writing about complex issues in novels rather than in nonfiction.

The novel is, and always has been, a self-made form. We read them as children, go on reading them, and then decide to try writing one, to see how our own experiences look on the page. Not all of my students will have enough luck (or maybe dedication) to write about their experiences and stories, and not all of them will find a publisher or an audience, but I hope that the ones who are really dedicated do so, because their depictions of one of the largest, most beautiful, most populous, most diverse, and most contradictory states in the US are revealing and fascinating.

Most of the essays in this book have been assignments—I am handed a topic and asked to reveal my thoughts. I hope that I have used them in the same way that I have used my novels—to learn more about something that I thought I understood, and to understand that topic, or issue, with more clarity and nuance.

My Absent Father

Our family abounded in tall, handsome veterans of World War II. My uncle Hal had been an army photographer—his job was to lie in the belly of US bombers and take pictures of the bombings, to make sure that the targets had been destroyed. My uncle Carl flew planes in the Pacific. My absent father was said to be cut from the same angular, dark-haired, hypermasculine pattern. The war may not actually have been a constant topic of conversation in my childhood, but it seemed to be, at least to me. These men stood up straight, as if still in uniform, and spoke in loud voices, as if still giving orders.

But, around the time of my first birthday, in 1950, my father was placed in a veterans' hospital with some sort of mental disorder, which may have been schizophrenia or may have been PTSD or may have been something else. For a year and a half after my father went into the hospital, I lived with my mother's parents in St. Louis while my mother stayed in Michigan, attempting to understand their future, her future, and my future, and so my father became a fictional character—portrayed by my mother in detail and with a tragic air. He was uniquely handsome ("Gregory Peck"), brilliant, and charismatic. He had gone to West Point and chosen the cavalry—but the cavalry was disbanded, so they put him in the tank corps, except that he was too tall for a tank. He turned to the Army Air Forces, but because he was too tall for a plane, he invented a way of refueling planes in midair. When they tested his "hypodermic method," one of the testing planes crashed and the pilot was killed. While my father was working out the kinks, the British came up with another method, and he found himself back in the infantry. He was sent to Bavaria to organize and aid the sea of refugees then flooding in from the east, and there he met my mother, who was serving in the WAC. The army and the war provided the grand backdrop for my father's dramatic episodes of bad luck, but he did not fit in there.

When my father did visit, when I was four, he filled our one-bedroom apartment with his resonant voice and his 6′4″ frame. I found it strange that he was there in bed with my mother (where I often nestled or played or chatted) and strange to see his possessions on the bathroom counter. I felt a hovering shift in the atmosphere that denoted that things would soon be done differently around here, and an answering feeling of dread. My father didn't have a lot to say to me, but one morning he called me over to him when I came out of the bathroom, turned me around, and pulled down my pants to see whether I had wiped myself properly. The rest of the visit remains hazy—maybe because the hygiene incident was so vividly unprecedented. I do remember him showing us how to work the new television.

My parents were divorced shortly after the visit, but my mother continued to tell me about my father's dashing genius. His uncle, a Michigan state legislator, had gotten him into West Point after misadventures elsewhere. At West Point, he was almost cashiered for insubordination several times. At the end of the war, he got a general discharge instead of an honorable discharge. When my mother and he ended up in Los Angeles, in the late forties, he could not find a job—my mother earned their daily bread. The implication of this latest fact might have been that his problem was unusual. Although unemployment among veterans was generally high, perhaps potential employers could sense that he would be hard to handle and arrogant. But another possibility was always there in my mother's stories—maybe he was just too good for them. When I was ten or eleven, she found a photograph from the newspaper announcement of their marriage. Since she'd been working for that newspaper at the time, it was a large picture, full length. She looked like Ingrid Bergman, and he looked like, yes, Gregory Peck. The article was dated December 7, 1948. This time, she told me how he had wooed her with ideas for all sorts of brilliant inventions, which he had lost interest in prematurely. It was he who had bought my innovative baby bottles—they were right out of *Popeye*, the nipples at the ends of long hoses. For a while, we did have a few items around the house that he'd thought were brilliant—for example, a record player for 45s; 33s, he thought, were going nowhere. Really, though, he preferred the wire recorder to the tape recorder, fidelity and purity over convenience. As for my mother's aspirations as a writer, my father told her that writing was for "second-rate minds"—a novel, for example, could never be as well written as the Army Field Manual. She seemed to forgive him this prejudice—he was just so compelling.

My mother got full custody of me, and I later learned that my father had a habit of driving to St. Louis, then up and down my grandparents' street, hoping to see me. My grandmother was adamant—she sent him away. I remember his arriving only one time. Perhaps I was seven. I was happy to see him, in spite of the toilet-training incident. He was still handsome and still had that fictional extra dimension that my now domesticated uncles lacked. I sat on his lap on the front porch of my grandparents' house for a bit while he chatted with my grandfather in the other chair. My grandmother watched from just inside the screen door, and then my father walked down to the street and got into his car.

•

As the years went by, I stopped listening to stories about my father, stopped paying attention to the murmurs of compassion for me as a fatherless girl. I took my uncle to father-daughter night at school, and I viewed the fathers of my friends with some skepticism—they seemed tall and vapid, much less dynamic than the mothers. Thinking of my father made me nervous, but I did visit one set of cousins. They were nice; they had a boat; they were well behaved and circumspect. When my uncle, my father's youngest brother, spoke, he made pronouncements rather than jokes. The relationship went nowhere.

The traditional Freudian interpretation of how boys and girls grow into sexuality is based on Greek myths—Oedipus, Electra—but as soon as I read those myths (in eighth grade, in Edith Hamilton's *Mythology*) I sensed that they had nothing to do with me, a child of divorce. I did have a complex, though, one I call the Tom Sawyer complex. The great boon of my childhood was my boy cousins. Jody was almost three years older (born in November 1946), and Steve was two years older (born in July 1947). They were dynamic and handsome, and I couldn't take my eyes off them.

My grandparents' house was where we gathered, and my grandparents let the boys run free. My grandfather had grown up a bit wild, in the 1890s and 1900s, and though our parents recalled him as very strict, by the time we came along, those days had passed. My grandfather was more interested in playing golf and making jokes, and my grandmother liked baking and gossiping with her friends and neighbors. Their house was comfortable rather than stylish, filled with my grandmother's crocheting and embroidery. If my grandmother ever yelled at us, I don't remember it—the most she ever did was throw her hands in the air and tsk. My grandfather had a hotter temper, but, especially with the boys, he was playful and teasing.

The boys climbed on roofs and clambered up trees; they put pennies on the railroad tracks and firecrackers under tin cans. They threw water balloons out the front window of my grandparents' house, and they sledded down the steepest hills. They told me things (that I could not, in fact, marry my mother; that everything on the back of a cereal box was true; what a Communist was; that a bird ate seven times its weight every day) and showed me things (a German helmet that my uncle Hal brought back from the war with a hole where the shell fragment went through, the difference between a flush and a straight, why you couldn't get a plain hamburger at McDonald's). They took me places (to the swimming pool, on the Round Up at the carnival, downtown to the drugstore, to their friends' houses where strip poker was being played—sort of). They propounded theories, fell asleep in front of late movies, stayed up all night. They were always on the go, but they were always nice to me, maybe nicer to me as their cousin than they would have been if I had been a pesky little sister.

When I was eleven, my mother remarried. My stepfather was portly and kind, too old to have fought in the war. He was far more successful than my father would ever be. What he did in the world—run a small petroleum company, oversee his own children as well as his birth family, travel to the Middle East and Venezuela, build a house for my mother, and allow me to buy my first horse—was saintly but not mythic. I am sorry to say that this image of kindliness and success did not form the iconography of my desires.

My new stepbrother, Bill, though, was the same age as my cousins, just as good-looking but with a Catholic twist—he wore his hair in a ducktail with long sideburns, he smoked, and he was always working on the engine of his '56 Chevy. He was as wild as they come, a good girl's dream older brother, who climbed out of the upstairs window when he was grounded, had passionate girlfriends who called and came over day and night, and wore a permanent half smile, as if the joke of existence was always being freshly told. The Tom Sawyers were a threesome now, brawny and daring, handsome and on the move. If one didn't have a motorcycle, another one did. The cops, the narrow escapes, the pieces of good luck, the sparkling blue eyes, the irreverent laughter were features of all their adventures.

When I left home to go to college, I was thrilled to discover that Tom Sawyers abounded, and that they were neither cousins nor stepbrothers. Just like the boys back home, they had theories and ambitions. If they were not in trouble at the moment, they recently had been in trouble, so they had stories to tell. And just like my cousins, they never even thought of restricting my freedom. There was a girl in my dormitory who told me that her boyfriend wouldn't allow her to come out of her room unless her hair, clothing, and makeup were perfect—slavery. I wore what I wanted to wear, and if that included belting my navy surplus jeans with a string, well, I liked the effect. My boyfriends egged me on: Let's live in a Marxist commune and talk political theory day and night. Let's work in factories or hitch-hike to Cape Cod or drive a clunker from New York to St. Louis. Let's go to Europe for a year with only our backpacks. Let's work on an archaeological dig. Let's get lost. Let's drive the motorcycle a thousand miles (including the mere six hours from St. Louis to Cleveland), and when it gets stolen let's hitchhike home. Let's live in a ramshackle cabin and forage for heating wood. Let's take the band on the road, let's live on 260 dollars a month, let's drive to California and up the coast to Oregon and back home. Let's get pregnant, let's start a family—what could go wrong?

•

Eventually, I became gainfully employed and the author of two novels. In the fall of 1983, one night when my husband was away and my daughters had been put to bed, I was unaccountably seized with thoughts of my father. I went to the phone and called information for the town where he lived, and tricked them into giving me his address. The next day I sent him *Barn Blind* and *At Paradise Gate*, my first two novels. I toyed with enclosing a note, decided against it. I didn't know what to say, for one thing, and I wasn't sure how big a step I wanted to take toward acquaintanceship, for another. I was a little relieved when there was no response, and I forgot about it until two months later, when I got a call telling me that my father had died, leaving me his only heir. The caller was a woman my father had known— the circumstances of his passing were mysterious. His friends suspected that he had starved himself to death, as he was prey to numerous anxieties about food. Or, they thought, maybe the hospital had let him die because he refused treatment. His abode was a mobile home, so full of books and pamphlets and other debris that it sagged on its foundation. Did I want to come and go through all the stuff?

I did not. I felt even less about the death of my father than I expected to feel—not only no sense of loss but also no curiosity.

And, by the way, a copy of one of my books was found in his bed. He had been reading it the night they took him to the hospital—this struck me as eerie but not moving. I knew he was a curious man—I gave it no more meaning than that.

In the end, they sent me his car. It was a Datsun, full of little gadgets that plugged into the cigarette-lighter socket. A pair of his flip-flops, very large, was under the seat. The carpeting was sandy. It was as if he had just gotten out of the driver's seat and gone into the house, a patch of Florida in the midst of an Iowa winter. I sold it and bought a station wagon, but not before retrieving from the trunk a steel file box full of photographs, some identified and some mysterious— Was my father's father really the youngest of twelve? Really the son of a photographer from Rock Island, Illinois, who seemed to have taken the photos (including several of himself tipping his hat to the camera)? The possible great-grandfather had the look—tall, lean, bald, bespectacled. The most mysterious photo in the box was of a weather-beaten, unsmiling fisherman, taken in Nova Scotia. Was that where they came from—Glasgow to Canada to Illinois, hardscrabble all the way, until one of them, the youngest, the one with his arm around the dog, married into a dynasty?

All the Tom Sawyers settled down. Bill became an accountant. Steve became an editor. Jody completed his service in the navy and went to work organizing large construction projects. They replaced their wild ways with self-knowledge and responsibility. Their avatars, the ones I married and had children with, made similar transitions. White-haired now, but still fun and funny. Our children are the same age that I was when I was glorying in our freedom.

A few years ago, after several decades of not saying much about my father, my mother remembered another story. They were living in Los Angeles. My mother was pregnant with me. They were walking down the street, and he suddenly grabbed her hand and took her into a Catholic church, where he went up to the altar and knelt down. My mother was both surprised and alarmed—normally, my father was vociferously opposed to religion, his acknowledged deities being science and technology. But he knelt there for a fairly long time, and seemed to be praying. When he stood up, he took her to him and said, "You have been given to me as my handmaiden."

I can easily imagine my mother, looking like Ingrid Bergman, recoiling from this role. My grandparents hadn't raised their ambitious eldest daughter to be anyone's handmaiden. But I was about to be born; my mother had committed herself. Maybe she thought it would all turn out okay. And it did, though not in a way that anyone could have foreseen.

Because my father gave me two precious gifts. One of them was his height. The height was the surprise. All through elementary school, I was the same size as my friends, sometimes half an inch taller or shorter, sometimes a couple of pounds more or less. I fit in with the crowd in the most obvious ways. When they weighed and measured us at the beginning of seventh grade, I was about the same as the other girls, 5′1″ and 100 pounds. Two years later, I was six feet tall and 125 pounds. My mother was so worried that she sent me to a growth specialist, and he estimated what was to come. He was right—between ninth and tenth grade, I grew another two inches and gained twenty pounds, and then I stopped and awakened from a growth-induced haze. I can't say I minded being so tall. There were models my height—I had a picture of Veruschka on my mirror. She and Vanessa Redgrave were a two-person example for tall girls of how to get ahead. Usually, Veruschka and Vanessa were photographed alone, in a park, on a street or forest road, so that's what I thought tall girls did— they made their way, free and strong.

•

But my father's gift of absence—I've come to realize that that was even more precious. Because I have children of my own, I have theories and beliefs about raising children, and one of them is that a man who pulled down his daughter's pants to check her hygiene would have had a role for me to play (maybe handmaiden, maybe something else) and a standard for me to live up to. He would have seen me as a reflection of himself, and as his self became more desperate and disorganized, his demands on me would have intensified—the world is full of men who, once they have lost power over their colleagues or their lives, redouble their power over their families. He would have made sure that I knew that I was female, and that females have limited capacities and defined roles. He would have disdained my failure to grasp, say, algebra, and my devotion to the Bobbsey Twins and Nancy Drew. Unlike my grandparents, he would not have been wise enough to leave me alone, and unlike my mother he would have been idle and looking for a project.

About a year ago, one of my cousins on my father's side said that he, his sisters, and another cousin were coming to California and would like to meet me. I was cool to the idea, but I did think that the metal box of old photos belonged more to them than it did to me.

We met in Los Altos over a long breakfast, and they were not only charming but affectionate and supportive of one another. I admired them. They had, indeed, suffered the difficult childhoods that my grandmother had been determined to protect me from, but they had also benefited from years of therapy and years of scrupulous honesty. And they loved my father, who had befriended them and saved them when their own parents, his sister and her husband, failed them. To them, he was kind, good-natured, and funny. And my cousin told me a story about visiting my father in Florida. They were all in their teens. One day, he took them to his favorite beach, and after they laid out their towels and umbrellas he went over to a tree and set his loafers at the base. Into the heels of his loafers he put a few nuts, then he called out. I don't remember the names he used, but let's say Lucy and Desi—something amusing like that. Pretty soon, a pair of gray squirrels appeared in the upper reaches of the tree, looked at everyone. My father backed away, and the squirrels skittered down the tree and ate the nuts in the shoes, and also a few more that he gave them by hand. A nice man.

I enjoyed this story, but even so, I don't feel that I missed anything. I know from my own experience as a parent that sometimes it takes disappointment and heartbreak, as well as a little distance, to disabuse you of your cherished notions of who you are, who your child is, and how you might "mold" him or her. When my father knew me, he seems to have been both confused and very sure of himself, a fearsome combination.

The Tom Sawyers made chaos and distracted my mother, stepfather, grandparents, aunts, and uncles. This gave me the private space of being a comparatively good girl, where I thought my own thoughts and came up with my own ideas. A girl who is overlooked has a good chance of not learning what it is she is supposed to do. A girl who is free can grow up free of preconceptions. Sometimes, from the outside, my work and my life look daring, but I am not a daring person. I am just a person who was never taught what not to try.

Iceland Made Me

The thing you want to remember most about going to Iceland is all the hiking you did, up the hills and across the dales—wind, rain, and sunshine poured over you and through you, but you were always facing down the elements, maybe with the aid of a little hat and a poncho. You will have knitted your own socks from oily (but natural) Icelandic wool, and your own gloves, too. Your backpack will have contained dried reindeer meat for sustenance, a few containers of *skyr* (like yogurt), and, because you were so adventurous, some *hakarl*, which is shark meat allegedly buried in the sand and then preserved by fishermen who urinate on it as they go by every day for a few months, until it is truly inedible to everyone but Icelanders. You will not have had even a sliver of *rjomaterta* (cream cake) in your backpack because you were too sturdy for that, and your only reading matter was by medieval saga writers. (Halldor Laxness was way too modern for you.)

But I am unlike you—my main memory from my eight months in Iceland is sleeping. My favorite dream was of myself swimming in the waters of the north Atlantic (unrealistically warm and bright), and being approached by a pod of dolphins, who lifted me out of the water as they leapt into the blue sky, then let me down gently to float again in the gentle sea. Almost all of my dreams were more vivid than any I had ever had, and from them I understood some of the incidents in the Icelandic sagas—for example, the monster who sits astride the roof of a house in *Grettirs Saga*, and rides it until the roof beams crack. As the nights grew longer and the days shorter (down to two hours in December), I remained on American East Coast time—I would go to sleep around four a.m. and get up at dawn (one in the afternoon), go swimming at the local pool (hail and ice on the concrete between the locker room and the hot tub) (the hotter one, not the hottest one, where the old men were boiling themselves and talking), then walk home in the dusk, stopping at the American consulate to take a book from the library, something I had never read (*The Grapes of Wrath*) or never heard of (*The Man Who Loved Children*, by Christina Stead) or was long enough to require many dark hours of concentration (*Anna Karenina*).

Iceland made me.

I was always a traveler. My earliest journey I do not remember—my mother and father driving from LA to Michigan when I was a year old—but I think I remember all of them after that—from St. Louis to Chicago on the train with my grandmother, to visit cousins when I was three, to Grand Rapids around the same time, to visit the other grandparents, down to the Current River in southern Missouri when I was nine and ten, then to camp in northern Wisconsin and Vermont when I was eleven, twelve, and thirteen. Always staring out the window of the plane or the train or the backseat of the car, fascinated by the landscape, listening to people around me talk. When I was a senior in high school, my parents let me go to England for two weeks during spring vacation, and that's where Iceland was planted, right there in those cathedrals and those dialects that my very saintly hosts exposed me to, day after day. After college, there were no jobs, so my first husband and I scraped together three thousand dollars and went to Europe for a year, first working on an archeological dig in Winchester, England, then hitchhiking through France, Italy, Greece, Crete, Yugoslavia, Austria, Switzerland, France again, Denmark, and back to England. He was 6'10", my mentor and protector. We met other travelers who had been scammed and robbed and frightened. The closest we came to being taken advantage of was in an Italian train station, where we fell asleep on some benches, and my husband woke up just as a man was attempting to steal his shoes from under his head (size sixteen—maybe they were worth something on the black market?) Much more typical was our experience at an outdoor bazaar, where we ponied up the asking price for some item, and the seller took pity on us. He taught us how to bargain, then gave us the item half off. In grad school, my boyfriend and I thought nothing of heading out of Iowa to California, Oregon, Idaho, New York, or Martha's Vineyard, by car or motorcycle.

But until I went to Iceland, I had never traveled alone.

There were seven or eight of us—my fellow Fulbright recipient, Elizabeth, and other students from England, Denmark, Norway, and even the Soviet Union. (He said his father was in the KGB, which was why he was allowed to leave—he also knew how to knit, thanks to his grandmother, so he fit right in.) Elizabeth had gone to Radcliffe and graduated summa cum laude. She had grown up in the Upper East Side of Manhattan and read *War and Peace* when she was ten. We got along well. While I was catching up on classics, she was plowing through Barbara Cartland. The Danish boy (four years younger than I was) was Knud. He was handsome and personable, with blond hair and a square, open face. He was a whiz at Icelandic—not all the Danes were. There was a woman who knitted in the lobby before class who was rumored to be stuck between the liquid pronunciation of Danish and the harsher, multiconsonantal pronunciation of Icelandic, unable to go either back or forward. She knitted like a whiz, though—the whole front of a baby's sweater in twenty minutes. Elizabeth and I lived in a dorm at Haskoli Islands. From the front door, you could see the mountains beyond Reykjavik rearing into the sky, crusty and barren. Once, I was sitting at my desk, and three swans flew by outside the window, close enough to touch, it seemed. An American professor was in Iceland on a teaching Fulbright. His name was Oscar, and he hosted informal parties every Sunday, where we ate the food he liked to cook, chatted, and played Hearts or Whist. What was eerie and alluring was the walk to his house, along the dark beach at night (it was always night), listening to the water lap the sand, to the wind slithering here and there. Oscar liked to bake, but Iceland was a treasure of baked goods so buttery and creamy that for the first time in my life, I had to pay attention to how often I gave in to temptation.

It was an easy walk to downtown Reykjavik, and I loved to observe the Icelanders, who spoke loudly and stood closer to one another than New Yorkers. My favorite episode was at the local grocery store. I was walking past the meat counter. A woman customer and the woman butcher were looking at a plate sitting on top of the butcher case that contained two stalks of celery. The butcher said, very clearly, "SELL-ER-EE." Then the two women shook their heads slightly and shrugged. No idea what that green thing was for. The greatest difficulty when I went to the grocery store was bringing home eggs—no cartons, just plastic bags. I could not get more that three or four home intact. But the skyr was great, the granola was great, the precious oranges from somewhere far far away were great, and there were other vegetables, too, grown in Iceland, in thermally heated greenhouses. My fellow students were more gustatorily adventurous than I was, and even ate whale meat (which was cheap).

Occasionally, we went to the movies, if only to test our Icelandic, and many Fridays we went to the philharmonic hall, which was within walking distance, where we listened to the Icelandic Symphony Orchestra. At Christmas, I went to New York, where I stayed with a friend on the Upper West Side. The first morning, I sat up in bed, wide awake, thinking it was noon. The sun was pouring through the windows and it was eight in the morning. After Christmas in New York, I went back to Iowa for a few days, where my boyfriend broke up with me (not unexpected).

Now I didn't even have a reason to write letters. When I got back to Reykjavik, the days were getting longer, but I didn't notice. All I did was read and read and walk. In late January, I did get so depressed that the only book that could help me was a collection of humorous essays by S. J. Perelman that made me laugh in the bathtub while I was hiding out from the darkness and my shirked responsibilities toward my language class and my dissertation. At some point, one of those points that are so sunk in the endless passing of time, I started writing a novel, always from about eleven at night until about four, when I fell onto my couch/bed and continued to dream of what I was writing. It was set in Idaho, and concerned my grandparents and my grandfather's brother trying to start a ranch with a little money my great-grandmother had given them and their winnings from as many poker games as they could get into. The best episode was very Icelandic—my grandfather and his brother were caught in a blizzard and had to dig a hole in the snow. They saved themselves by lying in each other's arms until the blizzard covered them over and then subsided. My Idaho had no trees.

I wrote and read, read and wrote, went once a week to the best hotel in Reykjavik where I did eat rjoma-terta, a six-inch-tall wedge of layer cake, all the layers made of cream flavored with different liqueurs. The other meal I remember was a traditional Icelandic end-of-winter feast, *Þorrablót*, consisting of everything that traditional Icelanders would have found in their frozen storerooms at about the time when the grass greened up and the sheep were allowed out into the pastures. The most startling thing on the plate, to me, was the singed sheep's head (*svið*)—eyes restfully closed. I took one look and opted for one of the alternatives, maybe a roast chicken. Elizabeth ate everything on her traditional plate with relish, including the liver sausage and the *súrsaðir hrútspungar*, which were lambs' testicles cured in lactic acid.

The days got longer. The Fulbright Committee packed Elizabeth and me onto a plane and sent us to Berlin for a meeting with all of the European grantees. The hosts showed us around and invited us to appreciate the difference between West Berlin and East Berlin, then still behind the Wall. I did appreciate the difference, but not as they wanted me to—what I saw in East Berlin was some kind of patience—letting the ruins from the war sit there until someone came up with a better idea than replacing everything with chrome and neon lights. We were taken to Dahlem, were we visited the botanic gardens and a few of the museums. The best piece of art I saw was a Japanese scroll painting that ran along the entire wall of one of the galleries, the story of a single journey up mountains and through forests that unfolded as you walked past it, peering carefully at the trees and the rocks and the tiny figures. The principal difficulty of solitary travel, I decided, was not being able to turn to your companion, to say, "Look at that! I love that!" Whatever revelations were pouring into you and out of you, they were yours alone.

I felt this the following week, too, when I hiked in the southwest of England, a region John and I had missed in our months spent in Winchester, York, and the Lake District. Exeter, Dartmoor (which reminded me of the *Hound of the Baskervilles*), Newton Abbot, Dawlish—the place names, the wide landscape, the grass and blossoming trees and the wealth of flowers (going from Iceland to England in March is indeed a revelation) seemed to sink into me and disappear, escaping all of my attempts to capture the view, the fragrance, the warm feel of the air in letters or diary entries. When I read the old letters now, I am embarrassed at how desperately they grasp at the things I was seeing and try to push them into the minds of my recipients. When we returned to Iceland we had five weeks left, the sun was everywhere, and I went back to work, this time relating the tale of my grandfather winning a diamond ring in a poker game, giving it to my grandmother, who had no wedding ring, and then my grandmother losing it down the drain of the kitchen sink when she was washing the dishes.

I began preparing to go back to Iowa City. I would move into my ex-boyfriend's apartment, I would work on my dissertation, applying modern theories of literary criticism to the Icelandic sagas; I would continue my solitary existence and come to enjoy it as well as rely on it. Duncan asked me to go riding with him.

Duncan was an oboe player from Edinburgh who had by that time been in the Icelandic Symphony for two or three years, though he was a year younger than I was. He was maybe the only person I knew then who was gainfully employed. He was also handy (he did, after all, have to make his own reeds, and they had to be good). He was outdoorsy, he was adventurous, and he had a car. In the last three weeks (now April and May, sun up at four, down at nine or ten), we drove to Dritvik, Laugurfell, Hlitharendi (the setting of *Njalssaga*), and Eyjafjallajökull. We saw Skógafoss, and stayed in a youth hostel near Bergþórshvoll. The grass in every valley was brilliantly green. On our second morning in the hostel, another Brit arrived—a sailor taking a break, as I remember. The two men talked all day about sailing and life on the ocean, and never once acknowledged my presence, which was an illuminating experience, the first time in my life as a 6'2" American woman that I was entirely overlooked. Which is not to say that Duncan was unkind. Every time we met for those three weeks, he had a plan or an idea about something that might be fun to do. He also had a lot to say about Scotland, the oboe, the orchestral life, music, nature, haggis, his former plan to sail from Scotland to Iceland to Greenland to America by himself. He wore glasses, his hair was red, he was as easygoing as any man I had ever known. We knew that our relationship was neatly circumscribed by my imminent departure. He didn't ask me to stay, and I didn't ask him if I could. What Iceland had to offer me was strangeness, the theme of seven and a half months on my own now gently expanded by his knowledge and mobility. My vocation, I knew, was to return to America and keep writing, but now I had Iceland deeply engraved into my own sensibility, not only by the land and the people I met but by the ghostly presence of the saga writers and the living Icelandic writers whose work I read, most notably Halldor Laxness, who was still alive and writing not far from Reykjavik, but whose books, especially *Independent People*, entered into me as if they had existed forever.

On the way home, we flew over Greenland. The sky was clear, and I stared down at the glaciers and the icy coast, fell more deeply into my fascination with that far-flung offshoot of Nordic restlessness, and arrived in New York, where the first movie I saw was *Annie Hall*, than which no film is less Icelandic, and the first food I ate was a bagel with lox and cream cheese from Zabar's, Icelandic in a much-translated but still evocative way.

I went back to Iowa City. Now, when I wrote, I was looking out the window at green grass and the white siding of the Foursquare house next door. I kept on with the grandparents in Idaho, my mother as an adventurous two-year-old wandering among the cattle while my grandmother cared for the new baby in the house. But I knew that the work to come, whatever it would be, had taken on a deep Nordic tinge, let's say a combination of wind and sky and snow and grass, of making the best of isolation and hard work, tragedy, luck, and magic.

Can Mothers Think?

The first summer I taught at Iowa State, my 8:30 class was across the campus from my office, and I walked there briskly every day, across the grass, through the trees, and over the fences, rather than along the walks. I was seven months pregnant, thirty-three years old, and I needed to feel that this wasn't the end of my tomboy youth. I taught modern fiction, including five days of Kafka—"A Hunger Artist," *The Metamorphosis*, "A Country Doctor," "In the Penal Colony." I wanted to imbue my fourteen undergraduate students with the enthusiasm for Kafka's work that I had, for its richness of meaning, its mysteriousness, its elusiveness. I remember, though, that it struck me one day as I was climbing one of those fences that it was very strange to be teaching Kafka and to be pregnant at the same time, pregnant by choice. My first thought, one of those superstitions of pregnancy on the order of rabbits and harelips, was that the child would be affected. I managed to set that one aside.

But I did not manage to resolve the uneasiness I felt at suddenly finding myself to be a living paradox, simultaneously carrying and professing hope and despair, in my head a devoted modernist, in my body a traditionalist of the most basic kind. Such a thing seemed clownish at least, and maybe impossible at worst.

And, since the early 1970s, feminist literary historians have been exploring the lives of women writers, seeking to understand the relationship between pen and gender, between literary production and human reproduction. This relationship has generally been found to be a hostile one, and the hostilities have been traced to many sources, including but not limited to notions of the pen as "a metaphorical penis"; creation as "an act of Godlike solitude and pride"; the triviality of traditional women's education; feminine habits of submissiveness, modesty, and selflessness; female anxiety about authorship; and of course the demands of family, domestic, and social life. As a young writer, I wasn't aware of all the obstacles in my path, but I didn't need scholars to tell me the basic and irreducible fact that all the authors I had spent my life admiring and emulating—Eliot, Woolf, Austen, the Brontës, Emily Dickinson—were childless, if not, indeed, also without husbands and lovers. The writers I knew of with children wrote books like *Please Don't Eat the Daisies*. The acme of *motherly* wisdom seemed to be Erma Bombeck. Even so, my goal since college has been to become not a popular humorist but a novelist of "grace, power, and wisdom."

When I first started writing, I avidly looked for signs and portents of the future. This went beyond astrology, beyond staring at my palm trying to decide if my "fame" line was actually well defined or not. If I want to recapture what raw ambition felt like, I remember how I used to read biographies of authors as possible maps for my own life. I read them with fear and longing. Those lives didn't seem very happy, very enlarged by art, very well integrated, or even, for that matter, very much fun. Clearly the wages of modernism. And I was a devoted modernist. I knew that the path to great artistry was as well defined in these biographies as the concrete walks between the buildings at Iowa State. The monuments of modernism and postmodernism distributed along the path were easy to see. There were writers then who frightened me, who liked to say, you'll never be a writer if you (fill in the blank) or if you don't (fill in the blank). I listened to them as avidly as I inspected that fame line or read those biographies.

Okay. I chose to be a writer. I had chosen to have one child. So far, so good. Alice Walker had chosen to have one child. She defended her choice in *Ms.* magazine. But, as far as I knew, she had not chosen to have a family of children, and here I was pregnant a second time, dividing myself even more deeply from the main body of admirable women writers. And here, in the summer of 1982, was Kafka. "In the Penal Colony," eerily prefiguring the Holocaust, was about torture. "A Hunger Artist" was about chronic failure to find satisfaction in the world. *The Metamorphosis* was about the experience of the self as an insect. And behind these were the other readings in the course, none of them hopeful about parent–child relations—*Native Son*, *To the Lighthouse*, *The Man Who Loved Children*, *Seize the Day*. Once I had read and understood and loved them, once I had bought what they had to say, could I repudiate them for *Please Don't Eat the Daisies* just because I was pregnant? That seemed a lot like a deathbed conversion to me, panicky and intellectually dishonorable. On the other hand, could I read them aloud to my children, bedtime stories about how real, serious, thinking people saw the world I was bringing them into?

Does such uneasiness engage a woman writer more than it does a man? To answer this question, I polled two of my colleagues at Iowa State, Joe Geha, whose collection *Through and Through* was published in 1990 by Graywolf Press, and Steve Pett, whose novel *Sirens* appeared in 1990 from Vintage. Their answers were more interesting than I had expected them to be. Yes, each of them said, he had felt a strong contradiction between aspirations of literary greatness and having children. Both felt uneasy about introducing a child to the modern, and modernist, world that we live in. Joe, however, found himself letting go of this contradiction when his wife became pregnant with his first child. He had lost control over the issue—the die was cast, and real life, you might say, resolved things. Steve, too, strongly felt the contradiction, in spite of the existence of two sons, eleven years old and five years old. The contradiction is resolved, but not dissolved—Steve felt divided both spiritually (by a necessary optimism) and practically (by a choice to live a stable middle-class life) from a place where (I couldn't quite pin him down on this) a somehow greater, wilder, or freer art has its sources. Let's call that the Romantic position. Polling my colleagues was illuminating for me, because I had assumed this to be a female question. I see that alongside the female question is a more general one that has to do, perhaps, with the conjunction of seeing and choice. Every writer, man and woman, seeks to see truly. The true modernist or postmodernist vision is a vision of disintegration, disorientation, anxiety, anomie. And reproduction, since the invention of the birth control pill, is no longer visited upon one. It is a choice that all writers feel the weight of, male or female.

And yet what my colleagues had to say also highlighted for me the characteristically female question. On the one hand, I never felt, as Joe did, that once I was pregnant, the die was cast, or that the issue was out of my control. It seemed more tenuous than that for me. Along with and part of the fact of carrying the baby was the knowledge that the pregnancy could fail or could be brought to an untimely end. The pregnancy was not a choice made and done with, but an assertion of choice that got bulkier and more certain every day, but would not actually have being in the world until the crisis of birth had been successfully weathered. But this left aside the issue of middle-class domestic life. If I did not find it especially confining, was that because I was too dull to sense a place somewhere else, where a freer and wilder and truer art could have its sources for me? I was looking for signs—paths and portents.

No denying it, our literary culture is built upon the works of many women and a number of men (Kafka, Keats, Wordsworth, Whitman) who did not have children. One effect of this is clearly the notion that Steve Pett shares, that life without children provides a freer, and perhaps more disinterested, vantage point for passionate observation, that parents must be so whittled away by mundane, piecemeal concerns that a larger artistic vision is necessarily destroyed, or at least lost sight of. Steve said to me, "I don't think about larger existential questions as much anymore. Some days it's all I can do to figure out how to get everyone home at five o'clock." This wilder, freer art claims for itself a broader, more disinterested, and therefore truer truth. This is often accompanied by disdain for the middle class, for the safety and security that the middle class seems to seek, largely as a response to the perceived needs of children for safety, routine, stability, order, and the daily felt love of their parents. Ernest Hemingway's intense hostility toward Oak Park, Illinois, comes to mind, as does nearly everything Henry Miller wrote and stood for. Arguments with middle-class life are a convention of American literature.

But we can argue about the mix of fathers and nonfathers in our literary culture. More crucial, and perhaps less coincidental, it seems to me, is the extreme paucity of mothers, and of the tradition of a maternal vision. What do we know about mothers from reading our literature? We know two things only, it seems to me. We know what they look like, and we know what others feel about them. The figure of the mother, seen from the child's point of view, is a common one in literature, but its familiarity doesn't make it less mysterious or illusory, since every child's view of his or her mother is compounded of so many wishes and needs and resentments and fears, not to mention preverbal imprintings—the child's view must be unreliable. And then there are depictions of the mothers of one's children. Feminist literary scholarship has done an excellent job, in the last twenty years, of pointing out how these portraits, too, are compounded of male wishes and fears more than of reality. For an example, the interested reader need only look at the journals of John Cheever, excerpted in the *New Yorker* in 1991. It is obvious that most of the portraits of the women he drew in his stories grew out of a very partial, needy, and narcissistic vision of his wife, Mary.

To ask "What is a true picture of a mother?" is to ask also "How do people come to know 'what is true'?" The answer narrative fiction poses to this basic human question is "point of view." As we look back over the literary history of our culture since *Don Quixote*, one thread is easy to discern, and that is the emergence into written literary voice of previously "voiceless" classes, nationalities, races, and affinity groups. It is not that these groups had not had a literature, which I define as a systematic way of looking at and analyzing the world through language; it is that the emergence of this "prepublished" literature into the sea of print can be dated. My favorite examples of this are the explosion of Russian literature at the beginning of the nineteenth century and the emergence of Black American literature in the 1920s. Each of these changed the perception of "what is true" by giving eloquent voice to individual members of groups that had not been heard before, by bringing what had seemed alien into the realm of what the culture defined, through literary forms, as human. For the fact is that, through idiosyncratic voice and point of view, narrative literature highlights the experience of the individual, offers intimate contact with another experience, and circumvents the social differences that inspire hatred and alienation.

It means something, then, if mothers never speak in a literary voice, and if their sense of themselves as mothers and their view of those around them are not a commonplace of our written culture. It means, for one thing, that everyone in the culture is allowed, or even encouraged, to project all their conflicting fantasies, wishes, and fears onto the concept of motherhood, and onto their individual mothers and wives, which in turn creates of motherhood an ever-changing kaleidoscope of unrealistic and often conflicting aspirations and roles. Surely by now, for example, we are all familiar with the overlap in psychology's view of mothers between "coldness" and "overprotectiveness." There is, because these two categories overlap, no positive ground of "autonomy" and "loving-relatedness" that mothers can stand on. In the world of psychoanalysis, there is no space for mothers to have their own points of view about the demands their children make and whether these demands are realistic and able to be satisfied.

The failure of literature to include mothers also means that potential mothers, girls in adolescence who are often avid readers, have no variety in their models of mothering, and no model for articulating what it means to be a mother. Thus it is more likely that these girls will internalize those externally formulated projections of motherhood they find in their culture and discover, to their disappointment and frustration, that their "performance" as mothers is almost inevitably wanting. Such views are likely to be reinforced by the husband/father, who himself has no reality-based understanding of motherhood.

And the failure of literature to include mothers means that the delicate negotiation between responsibilities to self and to others, as represented by children and husband, but also by social networks of friends and coworkers, is never modeled for the culture at large. There are, certainly, many successful mothers who know themselves and their children, who understand the pleasures and the dangers of the world we live in, who make their way with courage and intelligence and good humor. Successful motherhood is a unique form of responsibility-taking, rooted in an understanding of competing demands, compromise, nurture, making the best of things, weighing often competing limitations, in order to arrive at a realistic mode of survival. A successful mother, we may imagine, is one who actually *looks at* her children and sees them, constantly weighing their potential against who they already seem to be, finding a balance that encourages them to live up to their best potential while not destroying them with impossible demands—while at the same time knowing the world they live in well enough to realistically judge how free they might be allowed to be without endangering themselves. Can a culture exist without such a strong model of responsible, realistic care?

Where were the mothers? Why *didn't* they speak up? Can mothers actually think and speak? If we look at Virginia Woolf and Vanessa Bell, it is the one who lived without sexual intimacy and without children who can't stop talking. Novels, essays, journals, letters—we are avid for everything she has to say. But the one who lived a passionate, sexual, childbearing maternal life is, as far as the literary culture is concerned, dumb.

Others have written about the practical obstacles to mothers' writing—the pregnancies, the lack of day care, the myriad ways maternal responsibilities have fed into the already strong prohibitions against women writing. But I think there is something else. Perhaps one clue about maternal silence is in everyone's childhood memory of asking *Mom* whom she loved best, asking her with anxiety and fear—she *might* say, or imply, she loved your brother best. You *might* detect in her tone evidence for your suspicion that such was the case. But there is also confidence, for this question is a ritual, and the ritual answers are "I love all of you the same" or "I love everybody as much as everybody else; I just love you in different ways." A reassuring answer. Surely, the child thinks, this can't be true. It isn't true of me. And yet *Mom* says over and over that it is true of her, so it must be true of her. Her love, unlike mine, is special, equal. It is *mother love.* The child is obscurely disappointed, too, because she senses that she hasn't gotten quite the truth. The effect, though, is that, as with anything simultaneously doubted and desired, mother love becomes something to be protected, never investigated, projected onto but never asked about or probed too deeply.

Where do mothers speak the truth? They speak it among themselves, over lunch or in groups. They laugh and confide, or cry and confide, that little Bobbie is driving them crazy, that Mary seems slower than the others, that (the greatest taboo) Angela isn't very pretty. They tell each other that Bob is too hard on the children and doesn't listen to them, and that it is clear that Bobbie's anger at this is approaching the breaking point. They ask each other what to do, and advise each other, on the understanding that judgment, in these conversations, is at least somewhat suspended in the common knowledge that everyone's kids give them trouble, and that if you judge me harshly now,

I could return the favor in a year or two when your kid is arrested for drunk driving. Mothers, that is to say, do think, and they are very realistic and practical about mothering, but theirs is a literature, like the literature of Russia before the nineteenth century or of American Blacks before the 1920s, that had not, when I became a mother, inserted itself very deeply into the print culture. To write about our own experience could lead us into, God forbid, analyzing our children and husbands, to belying the idea of maternal love that they depend on. To write about the world could reveal in ourselves despair, alienation, fear, anomie that could communicate itself to our children and damage them.

Others have noticed the nonmaternal orientation of literary culture. In *Narrating Mothers: Theorizing Material Subjectivities*, editors Brenda Daly and Maureen Reddy note in their introduction the almost universal "daughter-centricity" of even feminist writing: "We most often hear daughters' voices in both literary and theoretical texts about mothers, mothering, and motherhood, even those written by feminists who are mothers . . . paying attention mostly to the effects of current conditions of mothering on children's progression into adulthood." Much of the reason for this, they suggest, is political: mothers are seen by many feminists as too implicated in the patriarchal power structure, or as too "limited" a group—to theorize about mothers is to exclude other women. Many feminist daughters define themselves in opposition to their own mothers, rejecting the compromises they have made and perhaps fearing, as well, the compromises they, the daughters, find themselves making. I submit another, in my view more pertinent reason. Writing as a mother is simply too hard, even for mothers.

For the paradox of literary composition is that our work, even our most "realistic" work, is based on literary models. Life comes in as a corrective, but it is literature that tells us how to make literature. I experienced this very difficulty myself. I had submitted to my publisher the rough drafts of my two novellas, *Ordinary Love* and *Good Will*. Each of these concerned a parent, a mother telling her story and a father telling his. And in each I wanted to use a form that would, I thought, be characteristically female or characteristically male. In fact, the male voice and his story—linear, suspenseful, full of cause and effect and action—came to me in one draft, and my editor demanded very few changes. *Ordinary Love* was much more difficult. The form I wanted to use was not linear. The most secret and dramatic section occurred halfway through, not at the normal time of climax. And the story was not complete, I thought, until the children's voices came back to the mother, until she had been forced to hear their responses to her assertions. And the fact is, it was not just that my editor was stubborn and, I thought, untrained to read this sort of text; it was that through many drafts I did not know what I was doing. I did not know how to make this unfolding form of secrets and surprises work. I was forced to write at the outer edges of my powers of formal invention, though I could actually hear my narrator's voice very clearly. The models for *Good Will* were all laid before me, as old and venerable as literature itself. The models for *Ordinary Love* were not even within me. I had to think them up as I went along. It was hard work.

But there is even more behind the "child-centricity" of literature than these points I have suggested. For the fact is that we approach literature, especially great literature, in the same way that children approach their parents. Everything about our education and our culture encourages us to do so. Shakespeare's phrases are embedded in the language, as if God-given. We identify certain names with greatness—Shakespeare, Milton, Melville, Austen—before we can make heads or tails of their writings. By the time we have begun to understand what they are saying, it has already taken on the color of universal truth, akin to phrases like "Round John Virgin" or "hollow be thy name"— it makes no sense, but everybody honors it anyway. And western education is conducted very much on a religious model—we enter special places of learning, and listen to certified authorities interpreting the unchanging words of invisible and distant masters. We are told that while over in the scientific laboratories old findings and even theories are being superseded every day, here in the humanities buildings the truth doesn't change—the human spirit remains the same, a fascinating mix of good and evil, and delineated, never again so profoundly, by those who have gone before. There are even those who maintain that the language has been, somehow, at least partially used up. Writers of the Renaissance, they say, had the benefit of a robust new language. The tired old language we have now will never express such passion again. This idea makes me think of families where Dad and all the kids are served, then Mom makes do with the heels of bread, the bones from the leg of lamb, and some deflowered stems of broccoli. There are even those who insist that authors do not exist. In this case, Mom belatedly answers her invitation, and discovers that the banquet is entirely over, the tables have been sent back to the caterers, and a vociferous number of the guests insist that no one even ate. Mom is obliged to take her hunger and go home.

Most writers who are not deconstructionists read the same way children do, receiving the truth from printed texts, allowing those truths to scour our souls and find them wanting, and the easiest thing in the world is then to *write* as children, following forms and rules that provide a well-marked path to greatness. Such a well-marked path we find, for example, in the disintegration and anomie of both modernism and postmodernism.

It is harder to write as an adult. However little we defer to our own parents or other authorities, it is still tempting to defer to the authorities of the literary world and, if we teach, more than tempting to aggrandize ourselves by inculcating our students with belief in the greatness of the works we require them to read. But the trouble with greatness is that it seems to shade ineluctably into universality. When we assert that Shakespeare is the greatest writer of English, we can't seem to resist also asserting that his truths are the most universal. Another proposition that could be made, that his assertions are simply the most interesting and complex, doesn't satisfy our need to get next to the best, highest, and most important. Or, if we are of a different temperament, to deconstruct the best, highest, and most important.

What does this mean for mother writers? To be an adult mother is, clearly, to have a vision that differs fundamentally in its experience and possibly in its expression from that of an adult father. We know this instinctively, and it doesn't matter if the cause of this difference is nature or nurture. It only matters that the difference exists. In addition, an adult mother's vision offers a critique and a corrective on the vision of the father. Is there a family in the world where, when the kids complain about Dad, Mom does not offer some insight into his character, some perspective on his "universality"? Where she doesn't at least roll her eyes in quiet exasperation at certain absurd behaviors? Over a long marriage, Mom's vision offers a detached running commentary, equal in weight and significance to Dad's, whether that vision is expressed

overtly or covertly. In fact, her very separateness
from Dad asserts his particularity, his fallibility, the
boundaries of his authority. To be an adult mother/
writer would mean to challenge the universality of the
themes present in "child-centric" and "father-centric"
literatures, to challenge them perhaps without even
knowing it, to challenge them as a natural result of
one's carefully observed experience. Concomitantly,
thinking about, questioning, discussing the experience of motherhood would develop this vision and its
theory, as, over the last thousands of years, the patriarchal discourse has developed through the contribu-
tions of thousands of writers and critics.

What would such a vision contain? I give you the
examples of Toni Morrison's *Beloved* and Sue Miller's
Family Pictures. Two more different families than Sethe's
family and the Eberharts would be hard to find, yet
the drama of each of these books revolves around
the question of how to define mother love. In *Beloved*,
Morrison makes a strong case for infanticide being the
highest form of mother love in some circumstances. In
Family Pictures, Miller gives the best answer I have ever
heard to the "Who do you love best?" question. After
Randall, the son with autism, dies, Lainey, the mother,
and Nina, the sister closest in age to Randall, are
talking. Lainey says, "Nina, no one gets love without
some conditions. It's not in human nature to love that
way, even your own children. You want certain things
from them. You want certain things for them. I wish I

could have loved you, all of you, that much. But that's not in me. It's not in anyone." Nina says, "You loved Randall that way. Randall got that love." And Lainey says, "Oh, Nina, don't you think I wish I could have loved Randall with all those conditions? What a gift that would have been! It's the only kind I ever really wanted to feel. The other kind . . . who would want to feel it unless they had to?" Here is a vision of love to set beside all the myths of mother love—a love that is the particular expression of a particular personality and character, the idiosyncratic, real love of an imperfect self, not an impersonal, vapid ideal based on others' conflicting needs.

Surely another aspect of a mother's vision would be something that is another aspect of these novels: preoccupation with—insistence upon—survival, rather than the grand gesture of tragic death that ends so many masterpieces. There is, in western literature, what has to be interpreted as a refusal to go on, a willingness on the part of the larger heroes to vacate the mortal world through conflict, suicide, or a failure of the will to live. Need I add that there's always a mess to be cleaned up afterward that is not the concern of the dead tragic hero? A mother's vision would encompass survival, as it does in *Beloved* and *Family Pictures*, would encompass the cleaning up of messes.

But there is another question, as always: Can we write about motherhood without having experienced it? The imagination, asserting its sole claim to power, cries "Yes!" but my experience, and the experience of other mother/writers—that what we have been feeling and doing as we have lived as mothers is *not* familiar, is in fact something that we had not been prepared for by our reading—contradicts the claim of the imagination. The paradox is that I have found it easier to write from the point of view of fathers than from the point view of mothers. I have, in fact, found it harder to sift through and understand my experience as a mother than to understand my husband's experience as a father because I have repeatedly felt the absence of a theory of motherhood formulated and thrashed out by other mothers, and the theories of motherhood formulated by psychology have simply felt wrong, and irrelevant, if not destructive.

Times have changed, and they have changed since I was first beginning to write not so long ago. Now the majority of women writers that I can think of have children, sometimes lots of children—not only Toni Morrison, Sue Miller, and Alice Walker but also Louise Erdrich, Francine Prose, Sharon Olds, Maxine Hong Kingston, Maxine Kumin, Diane Johnson, Cynthia Ozick, Joy Williams, Meg and Hilma Wolitzer, Alice Munro, Alicia Ostriker, Grace Paley. And these writers often write about motherhood. It is no accident that this is a list of many who are generally acknowledged to be the most interesting writers of our time. Am I asking you to infer that a new literature, the literature of real, live motherhood, is inserting itself in our time, into the literary stream? You bet. Am I asking you to infer that it is as new and important in its way as any other new literature has been? You bet. For while the feminists are arguing whether motherhood is politically correct, and male novelists are worrying, as they have been at least all of my life, that the novel is dying, and the critics are asserting that the novel is deeply corrupt and the authors are dead, the mothers are busily, energetically, and prolifically exploring undiscovered territory within our own psyches, and therefore within the psyches of our readers, who are, as some of the letters I get attest, embarrassingly grateful. Have these mothers hammered out a consistent and self-conscious new vision yet? I don't know. I suspect it is too early to say. But they have revealed worlds that are new and old at the same time, worlds that we have never read about before but that we know are true.

·

And so I gave birth to my child, and Kafka hadn't affected her at all. I also, I found, gave birth to my subject, not the adventures of motherhood à la *Please Don't Eat the Daisies*, but the implications of daily power—the way in which one's sense of virtue and the desire to be good and innocent conflict with the daily exercise of power over the child. I never understood the interplay of love and power before I had children. I never knew what it felt like to have my actions magnified so enormously by the dependency of another. The intensity of my feelings, both positive and negative, was a certified surprise to me. In bad times, the strength I found to maintain some kind of stable routine, the faith I had in the simple value of survival, all of this came to me through my children. The honest way of saying it is that motherhood is not a simple Madonna picture, or a simple witch picture, but a hugely profound, complex, and, most important for a writer, *interesting* mix of evolving forces that challenge and change the self and the world. Imagining motherhood opens the door to imagining every power relationship, every profound connection. After my children were born, I felt, almost as a physical sensation, the nexus of their conflicting wishes, hopes, needs. Far from depriving me of thought, motherhood gave me new and startling things to think about and the motivation to do the hard work of thinking. For me, much of that thinking has been done through narrative fiction.

I have to admit that someone has suffered in the process, and it's been Kafka. While I am still deeply moved by much of his work, especially *The Metamorphosis*, I now see it as fascinating but particular, *his* vision, not mine, many-layered and humanly recognizable, but masculine, in some irreducible way. Shakespeare (should I whisper?) too. Even Dickens, my old favorite. Nor do I accept universality, and its partner simplicity, as a concept. Nor do I any longer wholly accept modernism. What I substitute is a picture of many women in a room, exchanging anecdotes of pregnancy and childbirth, all anecdotes simultaneously the same and different, the multifarious and the simple, the One and the many, existing together without canceling each other out. To me that is the particular and complex vision of life that by and large is missing from our culture, whose absence has led us to invest our substance in religious fanaticism, crop monoculture, capitalistic gigantism, political and military conquest, aggrandizement of the self above everything and everyone else. It is a vision that, if we can insert it into the stream of literature, may help our culture to pause so we can save ourselves and the world that cradles us after all.

The Most Important Question

In **The Decameron,** on the third day, Fiammetta tells a tale that Boccaccio took from a Latin version of the *Hitopadesha.* In it, a man tricks a married woman he has a passion for into meeting him at the public baths. There, in the dark, he pretends to be her husband and rapes her. When she discovers that she has been deceived, she has no recourse other than deceiving her husband, whom she loves—the shame and degradation belong to her, not to her rapist. If we read the *Guardian* or most newspapers, we recognize this story, reiterated 650 years on—or, for that matter, since the *Hitopadesha* is from the twelfth century, 900 years on. The deceived woman, Catella, knows what her rapist knows: that like young women we read about today, she will be punished or killed for having been deceived, no matter what her intentions. But so what? *Plus ça change, plus c'est la même chose,* we might say. Except, thanks to the most important question, we do *not* say that.

The most important question was posed by Marguerite of Navarre in the 1540s. She posed it, perhaps, at her favorite thermal spa, Cauterets, in the Pyrenees south of Lourdes. It was, "Can a woman know true love and retain her virtue?" Marguerite was the sister of François I of France, and the wife of the king of Navarre, a much younger man. She was a poet, a reformist, and an intellectual. She loved *The Decameron*, which perhaps seemed as old-fashioned to her as *Pride and Prejudice* does to us—a product of former times that could do with a rewrite. When she sat down with her friends and relatives to generate another hundred tales, she made two rules: the tales had to be true (in other words, gossip), and they had to answer the most important question. Marguerite died in 1549 before compiling one hundred tales. The seventy or so she did compile were collected after her death as *The Heptameron*. They are, in their way, a bit more interesting than the tales of *The Decameron*, because the conversation about each tale is longer and more probing than the responses of the tellers to the tales in *The Decameron*. The gist of the answer that Marguerite's tale-tellers eventually come up with is no: a woman cannot know true love and retain her virtue.

But in the late seventeenth century, the question was addressed again, this time by Madame de Lafayette in *The Princess of Cleves*. The princess of Cleves has a similar problem to Catella. She is married, properly and to a decent fellow, but another man, somewhat of a rake, loves her. As the story evolves, it turns out that the princess returns her lover's affections. She cannot act or demonstrate what she feels—she lives in the court of François I; eyes are always upon her. Marguerite's question suddenly falls into parts. What does it mean to know? What is true love? What is virtue? And perhaps for our purposes the most interesting, what is a woman?

To solve the riddle, Madame de Lafayette employs a literary device that playwrights cannot employ: free indirect discourse. She enters into the minds of her three characters—the wife, the husband, and the lover. She convincingly portrays their feelings and how they think of their feelings. She allows them to keep their feelings secret, and shows the pain and the pleasure of that secrecy. The princess does know true love (her feelings are convincing), and she does retain her virtue (she remains faithful to her husband and recognizes the difference between the erotic feelings she has for her lover and the affectionate feelings she has for her husband). Most important, she elicits the reader's sympathy for her dilemma, because Madame de Lafayette has successfully engaged our empathy—that is, she has enabled us to see things from the princess's point of view. Her feelings that cross the patriarchal red line do not offend us, because once we have experienced them, we cannot discount them. We are now connected to the princess.

Compare this to our experience of Desdemona in *Othello*. Shakespeare in some ways answers Marguerite's question, but his answer is much more circumscribed. Yes, we may say, Desdemona knows true love, at least for a while. She does love Othello, in spite of her father, in spite of Iago, in spite of being surrounded by warrior males. But what we know doesn't matter to Othello— he kills her anyway. Our job with Desdemona is to believe what she says, not enter her consciousness or experience the world as she does, though we are asked to hear the thoughts of Othello and Iago in asides and soliloquies. To sympathize with Desdemona is to do something simpler and more direct than to empathize with the princess of Cleves.

Let's return to the four parts of the most important question. What does it mean to know? What is true love? What is virtue? What is a woman? Other authors addressed these questions without upending, or even challenging, the patriarchal system. There is something about the way these questions entered the world after 1665 that gave us the world we have today, where women such as myself have a large degree of autonomy, active inner lives, and a constant sense of agency.

My favorite novel by Daniel Defoe is *Roxana*. Roxana is a prostitute who relates her own story, much as Robinson Crusoe relates his own story. She does not retain her virtue and, depending on our theory of true love, she does not know that, either. But she does know herself—that is the point of her confession—and she experiences herself, in the first person, as a woman and an agent. For many years she lives successfully in the mercantile world of property and sex, gaining a comfortable life and putting up with significant episodes of bad luck. She takes responsibility for her sins, and then she takes responsibility for her repentance. She wonders if she would have repented if she hadn't fallen on hard times and feared exposure.

Roxana was a very popular novel in its day, but not respectable. It kept getting reprinted and reworked by printers as a way of sorting out its moral ambiguities, but what lingers is not the downfall but the exuberant self-actualization (and survival) that Roxana manages in the difficult seventeenth century. Like *Moll Flanders*, also told in the first person, *Roxana* appeals to and expresses the inner life of women. And as soon as that inner life is expressed, it must be complex—it must be like the inner life of Samuel Richardson's Pamela, who spends five hundred pages fending off rape by her boss and writes down everything she can, even though she is a servant girl. A literate servant girl! A literate servant girl with an extremely detailed inner life! A literate servant girl whose tale sold like hotcakes! Talk about suspension of disbelief!

The thing is, Pamela knows very well what virtue is, what true love is, and what a woman is: someone with a voice and an identity, intentions, intelligence, and a will to defend herself. It doesn't matter that Pamela is Richardson's idea of a woman. He knows the readers he might appeal to—they are out there; they are literate women. And girls. They have money to spend on books. They are customers. Richardson the printer recognized that women authors might sell. He helped twenty-four-year-old Charlotte Lennox edit and publish *The Female Quixote*, and he also served as a mentor to Henry Fielding's sister, Sarah.

Authorship of novels was a good semiprivate gig for a woman. She could stay home and do it, she might make some money, and it was not quite as risky for one's reputation as being, say, an actress or a singer. Many women did it. One hundred years later, Nathaniel Hawthorne complained that "America is now wholly given over to a damned mob of scribbling women, and I should have no chance of success while the public taste is occupied with their trash—and should be ashamed of myself if I did succeed." He might have blamed Richardson. In the end, Hawthorne did not achieve wealth, but he did achieve the thing that his particular *bête noire* at the time, a novel by Maria Susanna Cummins (then in her twenties) did not—status. And the tension between the two has preoccupied novelists ever since then. What a luxury—if you have status, you can wish for sales, and if you have sales, you can wish for status. The squabble goes on today.

But why the most important question is important is revealed in the life and work of Daniel Defoe. Defoe's family were dissenters, fully involved in the religious and political tumult of seventeenth-century Britain—a period when, according to Geoffrey Parker in *Global Crisis: War, Climate Change and Catastrophe in the Seventeenth Century* (2013), printing presses all over the world started putting out thousands of pamphlets of discourse, theory, and agitation against governments that were failing in the face of famine, disease, social change, and civil unrest. Defoe lived through the Great Fire of London, the plague, and the attack upon Chatham by the Dutch. He was a merchant, and well traveled, and because of his religious beliefs, quite practiced at looking within. He worked as a pamphleteer himself, often writing fake confessions for criminals hanged at Tyburn. The sensationalism of his subject matter opened up the inner lives of those hitherto treated as objects and lured readers into empathy and shared experience, as well as thrills. In fact, the book trade not only opened readers to those experiences but created those experiences. In the US, a prime example is, of course, the great best seller *Uncle Tom's Cabin*, which enters the mind of Tom, sold down the river to pay debts, and also Cassie, a violated woman who plots revenge and escape. In the UK, a prime example is another great best seller, *Black Beauty*, an exploration of cruelty and the exploitation of horses, told by Beauty himself, that lives in the minds of millions of former little girls and little boys.

Pamela, *The Female Quixote*, *Uncle Tom's Cabin*, and *Black Beauty* all created controversy, and they did so in part because the novel is inherently political. A protagonist must exist in relationship to a group. There must be conflict between the protagonist and at least part of the group, and the conflict must be resolved in favor of, or in opposition to, the protagonist. Therefore the protagonist represents something, and what she or he represents is the exercise of power—her or his own, or the power used against her or him. The length of a novel means that with every turning page, empathy grows and the reader's commitment to the cause of the protagonist is likely to grow (otherwise he or she would stop reading). A long play lasts three hours. Reading *Tom Jones* or *David Copperfield* takes nineteen hours, at fifty pages per hour. And you think you are relaxing!

The most salient characteristic of being a reader is freedom, and this freedom is part of the political nature of the novel. Even when you are twelve years old and required by means of rewards and punishments to read *Oliver Twist*, you may stop. More than that, you may question and resist. How ridiculous is it that Oliver can't get a second helping of porridge? You decide. In fact, you must decide. You can decide that Oliver has suffered an injustice, you can decide that Oliver deserves his fate, you can decide that this can't possibly be true, you can decide that you do not care one way or the other, but whatever decision you are making, you are free to make it—there is no group disapproval, as there might be in a theater should you boo or get up and leave. The entire time you are reading any novel, you are experiencing freedom and autonomy, and this is a political experience. You are also experiencing either agreement with the author or disagreement, and this is a political experience too. He or she is luring you with plot twists, character development, pathos, wit, exotic scenes, but you decide whether to go along or resist. And there are resisters to even the most universally admired novels. A reviewer on Amazon writes of *War and Peace*, "The fact is that WP just isn't great, and we've been sold a bill of goods to make us feel guilty about falling asleep over it." After cataloging inconsistencies in the text, he concludes: "I agree with Tolstoy—it's a 'monstrosity.'"

Let's go back to *The Heptameron*. There they are, stuck in Cauterets because of seasonal floods. The ten storytellers have complicated relationships with one another, in a complicated era. The instigator of the game is the queen, but her mother is along and so is her husband, who always opts for the hypermasculine reaction—of course, if a woman is available, a real man will take her. The son of a cardinal represents the ideas of the church—but then, the queen is well known for being a reformist and aiding and abetting Protestant thinkers in Counter-Reformation France. One woman has lost her husband to the floods. There are two other couples; one of the men is notorious for his sexual prowess (and named Simontaut). There are five women and five men—disagreements could arise, because the material of the stories is about the relative power of men and women, and about what is right. Marguerite herself has a long history of being outspoken and valuing the outspokenness of men and women of conscience—in other words, although the ten storytellers must get along, they must also look within, and also be honest. They are, in this isolated world, allowed for the time being to be free. They are freer than the storytellers in *The Decameron*, because they discuss the philosophical implications of the stories in some detail, and they are more responsible, too, because they must tell stories that are real, not taken from other sources. They are, in short, being political while being personal.

But why is the most important question "Can a woman know true love and retain her virtue?" and not "Is every man free and equal?" It's easy to see that part of the reason is that the first question is a thin-edge-of-the-wedge sort of question. It does not seem to challenge the status quo, only to strive to understand it. Madame de Lafayette was writing around the same time that Blaise Pascal, René Descartes, and Baruch Spinoza were being censored for asking more aggressive questions about the meaning of life. It is also a question about half of the world's population, whereas the question of freedom and equality applies differently to different social and economic classes. It is not a simple question, but it is a question that a story or a piece of gossip can illustrate fairly easily. Without Marguerite of Navarre realizing it, perhaps, it is a question about possession: Who possesses a woman's virtue? Is virtue a thing? It investigates the heart of patriarchy without directly challenging it. When the king, as Hircan, continues to answer that any man who can take a woman's virtue can have it, the others contradict him. He moderates his opinions and is, in some sense, the first patriarch to be won over by empathy. Most important, it is a *question*.

I am not talking about greatness here, or how the most important question leads to great art. If we consider *Don Quixote*, we see that Quixote does not ask a question. He makes an assumption (or many assumptions). He goes out into the world, and his story is the story of putting his assumptions to the test—an early example of the scientific method, if you like. When Quixote and Sancho Panza meet people, they have discussions with them (Quixote sometimes goes to sleep if the discussion is about love), but the inner lives of the characters must be expressed in order to exist. We see from Madame de Lafayette that the essential variable for the development of free indirect discourse is the necessity of secrecy, which asserts that the inner life exists alongside the exterior life, in time with it, though not necessarily in tune with it. The inner life is the constant subject of the novel.

The most important question leads to entertainment, pleasure, ubiquity. The popular novel, as an art form, seems so benign, or even contemptible. Certainly, in Fielding and Sterne's day, a good girl was one who read sermons and poetry. But I would say a *smart girl* was one who read novels, who contemplated Pamela's dilemma, who went on to Fanny Burney, Anne Radcliffe, Susanna Rowson, and also Fielding, and also Sterne; one who read about the inner lives of both men and women, and who asked herself, through them, what is a woman, and after that, who am I?

I like to think of Madame de Lafayette going to a party, and running into a man there named Girard Des Argues, who was a mathematician and a theorist of perspective. I like to think of her subsequently looking at paintings and realizing that the use of perspective enlarges one person most of all, and that is the viewer, just as narrative enlarges the voice of the narrator. A narrator can be intrusive, and she can use a style that is very transparent or not at all transparent, but with every word that the narrator employs in the service of the tale she is telling, she inserts her perspective into the mind of the reader. The images the reader generates are given their subject and tone by the style, morality, and organizing principles of the narrator. Because the novel is prose, because it is in a book and therefore does not have to be memorized, the style of the narrative can be highly idiosyncratic. The classic tropes that narrative poets—especially poets who had to recite their works—needed to use to enable memorization and connection to other poems that were familiar to their audiences, are unnecessary and fall away. The novel is one-on-one. And the narrator, that poor slob from Paris (like Madame de Lafayette), but also from Clonmel (like Laurence Sterne) or Lynne Regis (like Fanny Burney), becomes an alternative consciousness for the reader during the reading and, if the novel is cherished, afterward, sometimes for many years (and I can always reread). Just behind the narrator, in the foreground of the novel, is the protagonist, whom I am viewing from within or without, or both, depending on the point of view that the narrator has chosen. The protagonist moves around within the imagined landscape, never ever overwhelmed by the heavens, the mountains, the buildings, the urban clamor, the great lords, or the government officials. In order for us to read about those giant things, they must be reduced to his or her perception and understanding, and incorporated into the experience of the protagonist. He or she may or may not prevail in the end, but merely by the act of organizing the experience of the protagonist into a lengthy comprehensible narrative, the author has outlived it, taken power over it, judged it.

What does this have to do with the most important question? It is a private, easily understandable, and readily accessible answer to the subquestion—What does it mean to know? To know means to investigate, to organize according to some sort of theory of cause and effect, and then to pronounce the protagonist's sentence in accordance with the justice or the injustice of the world that the protagonist lives in. It happens in great novels, it happens in hack novels—it supplies the reader (let's say she is twelve or fourteen) with the raw materials of her own theory of the world. When she goes to church, when she goes to school, when she sits at the supper table, when she hangs out with her friends, the theory she has constructed from her reading rubs up against the world she must deal with, and gives her opinions. From the outside, she looks like the girl you have known since the day she was born, who used to play with Barbies and now wears skinny jeans, but her inner life has become her own, has become a world of empathy and perspective that she got from reading novels. In her own mind, she is the agent of her own experience. It may be that she will not take kindly to an arranged marriage, to the circumscription of her rights in comparison to those of her brother, to her confinement to a small private corner of her sociopolitical world. I had this experience myself. When my daughter was eight and avid for Sweet Valley High novels, I read one after she went to bed, in which the bad twin falls off the back of a motorcycle and spends some time in a coma. In the morning, I said to Phoebe, "I don't really want you to read about this sort of trauma." Very informatively, she told me, "MOM! It's not trauma, it's DRAMA." Point taken.

How does this compare to other art forms, such as movies or music or pictures? Well, of course, the novel is not visual—the image I make of David Copperfield is not Freddie Bartholomew, at least until I see the movie, and then, possibly, I am offended that Freddie behaves so differently from my David. What I see in the movie is new and possibly illuminating information—a novel may try to give us the spectacle of the world, but films do it more efficiently and sensually. But it is spectacle, something seen and heard. It can arouse great feelings of sympathy and fear, but it pretty much fails at bringing me into the action, in spite of the music, in spite of the handheld camera, in spite of the slowing and speeding up of the film. No matter what else the director tries, he or she must fall back on showing me other people doing things. I must watch them, as I do in the theater. There may be less dialogue, because the actors have more leeway than they do on stage for demonstrating their intentions and emotions as they work them out across the landscape or, you might say, the cinemascape, but even as I go with them, I am seeing them as exotic, I am marveling at the difference between their experience and mine. The novel does the opposite thing, because there are no markers of strangeness. It asks me to discount their difference from me, and focus on their similarity to me.

It is much the same with painting, especially portrait painting. The great portrait painter looks at his subject, sees the true nature of that person within the appearance, and puts that knowledge into his painting, but the chances of me seeing those intricacies are very small. What I see is the artist's idiosyncrasies of style and vision as a veil between me and the subject, not an invitation into the inner being of the subject. Why is it not the same with novelists? Why does George Eliot's intellectual rigor and precision of style open up Dorothea and Rosalind and Lydgate and Casaubon rather than fencing them off? When I believe van Gogh, I believe that he sees the world in this way. When I believe George Eliot, I believe that the world *is* this way—at least for the space of *Middlemarch*, for the twelve hours it takes me to read the book.

The very length and silence of the novel makes it simultaneously ephemeral and intrusive—drip, drip, drip. I remember two characters in *Our Mutual*

Friend walking on the beach. They have tried to scam each other by getting married, and both have been scammed. Now they must scam someone else. Dickens describes the line in the sand left by the man's walking stick as a dragging tail. The image exists vividly in my mind, related to countless other images, thoughts, and feelings from the book, but also from the time that I first read the book (sitting beside a Christmas tree as a senior in college, living with four guys who couldn't find jobs); from other readings of Dickens; from authors I relate to Dickens, such as Trollope and Thackeray; from books I have read (and written) about Dickens's life; from thoughts I have had about Dickens's pride, prejudice, and good works. And it is only one novel. If I have read thousands of novels, then my inner life is full, teeming, accessible to me, expandable every time I return to *Our Mutual Friend.* Why would I ever let you control it?

Clearly, the most important question is one that is now unsettling the nonwestern world. Recently, in the *Guardian*, the girl Malala, whom the Taliban attempted to assassinate several months ago for her advocacy of education for women, reasserted her right to her books and her pen. Controversy lives in religious communities in the US, too, around the issue of God-given male dominance and female servitude. At the moment, I happen to be working on an introduction to the reissue of Rebecca Goldstein's *The Mind-Body Problem* (1983), in which the narrator's beauty and intelligence remove her, in the space of a very few years, from an Orthodox Jewish community in New York City to the philosophy department at Princeton—sixty miles and hundreds of years at once. She works out her fate in a fascinating novel. In his recent exploration of the world climate crisis of the seventeenth century, Geoffrey Parker points out that *The Princess of Cleves* is still in print, both on paper and as a Kindle book, still a part of the French national school curriculum. What is virtue, what is love, what does it mean to know, and what is a woman are achingly current questions. And I do believe that the novel cannot be replaced as a vehicle of learning by any other form.

Two days ago, I did a school visit. I asked whether any of the students had read *Oliver Twist* or *David Copperfield*. None of the students had, though most of the teachers had. Curriculums are changing. Perhaps the students are required to read other novels. I hope so. When I read *Oliver Twist* in seventh grade, I hated it. When I read *Great Expectations* in eighth grade, I hated it. When I read *Crime and Punishment* in tenth grade, I only understood the part about the horse falling to the cobbles and being whipped. But being required to read these difficult books prepared me to enjoy them when I became more proficient in the language of narrative. I went on to *David Copperfield*—loved it. Went on to *Giants in the Earth*—loved it. Went on to *The Scarlet Letter*—did not love it, but understood it and was amazed by it. I was the target, the books were the arrows my teachers were shooting at me, and some hit the bull's-eye and formed my sense of what I could do, what the world should be like, what is right and what is wrong. I see this in all my kids. We used to say that of the five kids, two loved to read novels, one wouldn't read a novel if her life depended on it, one would read a novel but only if his life depended on it, and one—well, we didn't know whether he *could* read. But now they are several years older, and the nonreaders have, surprisingly, come around. They tell us what they have learned from the novels they've read, and even though one thing they have learned is that we are ignoramuses, we are glad. They have learned to have their own opinions.

Marguerite, Queen of Navarre, Gives Desdemona Some Advice

This short story, based on the life of Marguerite, Queen of Navarre, was written in response to a request by the Folger Shakespeare Library to contribute to a series of chapbooks inspired by Shakespeare's works.

Vittoria Colonna to Marguerite de Navarre

Chère Madame,

I send you my fondest greetings and deepest thanks for your last epistle, which I received on the Feast of San Romualdo and have read several times since. I especially enjoyed the verses you sent along concerning the birth of your grand-niece to Henry the Dauphin and Madame Catherine de Medici. They are a fertile tribe, the Medicis. I write just now, not to share literary endeavors but to pass on a letter I have received from a young girl who is the daughter of a prominent merchant in la Repubblica Venezia. I have not heard that you, Madame Queen, have ever visited this place, but the customs are strange, as there is water everywhere and people of all sorts frequent the salons and man the army and navy. This laxity is the source of my friend's troubles. But I leave it to you, in your infinite wisdom of both the world and the spirit, to advise this young girl. I should say that she is some fifteen summers of age.

With great thanks, your devoted
Vittoria Colonna

Enclosed: Desdemona to Vittoria Colonna

Cara Madama Colonna,

I write you now because I need advice. When I met you in Orvieto, you seemed to be a kind woman, not unlike my own dear mother, who passed away when I was ten years old. You seemed to single me out, in spite of my common status, for special notice. This is what moves me to write you just now and seek your aid.

Some people would say that I have done a foolish thing—I have married the man of my own choice, without seeking my father's permission. I did not believe at the time and I do not believe now that permission for my marriage would have been forthcoming, and so I acted, and I have no regrets about doing so—my husband, Othello, is a loving and kind husband, a great general, and much revered by the Duke, but I believe that the only way that was open to me for achieving happiness was through a *fait accompli*. My father has become more and more opposed to the marriage rather than less. He says that this is because my husband is a Moor, but he is not officially a Moor—a Moor is a follower of Mohammed, and my husband renounced those beliefs when he went into service with the Duke as a young boy. If there is any problem with his beliefs, then it must be that he is of a reformist tendency (as you are, and I am), and he does not hesitate to question those ideas that many of us have come to doubt. It would seem that for the conservatives of Venezia, it is acceptable for a Veneziano to question whatever he pleases, but not for a Moor whose skin and eyes are dark, whose body is tall and graceful, and whose military skills are without peer. I have no doubts of my husband, but many doubts of those around him.

My immediate problem is that my father has gone before the Duke and accused my husband of witchcraft. Why he would do this, I have no idea— no taint of this sort has ever followed Othello. I suspect that the man who has poured this poison in my father's ear is an old suitor of mine named Roderigo, a hole-in-corner sort of fellow, wealthy but weak and complaining. He came to my father once and made an offer of marriage. My father said to me that in this life, marriage is about property and that

I should not be so foolish as to think otherwise, but I did think otherwise and I have earned my reward, which is joy and happiness. Please inform me, however, of some of the proper defenses against accusations of witchcraft. I will communicate these to my husband, and with luck, we can throw off these inconveniences.

Your fond and obedient friend,
Desdemona

Marguerite, Queen of Navarre, to Desdemona

Madame,

I hope that you will not reject the care and prayers of a woman whom you do not know, but who is your friend and well-wisher. My dear friend Vittoria Colonna forwarded to me your inquiries about witchcraft and disobedience. Perhaps this is because I have made something of a study of the relations between men and women, and I am, as well, deeply concerned with the teachings of our Lord Jesus Christ and the ways that they have been perverted to the uses of men. You must know, my child, that every man considers the daughter he has produced, or the wife he has taken, or even the woman he loves, as his own inalienable possession. That she herself might speak and assert a preference, he takes as an insult to his honor. Although in eloping with a fine and honorable man, you have done your heart a favor, you have also brought your honor into question, and more importantly, in a practical sense, the honor of your father and of the fellow Roderigo. These men can only conceive that you would give yourself to a Moor by means of witchcraft— every man is a victim of his own self-love— he cannot see another man as worthy of his beloved's affections. Othello's defense against accusations of witchcraft is his usefulness to the Duke—if the Duke trusts him and relies upon him, he will cast off these accusations. Othello, therefore, must continue to be the man that the Duke knows and understands, and the both of you must have faith in Our Lord Jesus Christ to preserve him.

I remain your well-wisher, and hope to hear that these difficulties abate as more important concerns replace them in the minds of your father and the Duke.

Yours in Christ,
Marguerite, Queen of Navarre

Desdemona to Marguerite de Navarre

Chère Madame de Navarre,

I cannot express to you, Madame, the gratitude and amazement that I felt when I saw your letter, and then read your kind and honest thoughts about my situation. I blushed to read your reprimand. I perhaps did not as carefully weigh my actions as I should have. My only defense is that my Othello is, indeed, not only the kindest and most loving of men, he is also full of knowledge and wisdom. In his service to the Duke, he has seen a world of people and places—his tales are exciting, and what he takes from them is wisdom itself. How could I resist this? And he came to me with greater love and respect than I had ever known from a suitor or, indeed, from my father or any other man. If this was not a man I could trust, then who is?

I have some support in my distress—my maid, Emilia, and her husband, a man named Iago, agree with me that everything will arrange itself, and that Othello is a natural prince. In the past, I have found this Iago a slippery and cold sort of fellow, and in fact I was unsure about taking Emilia for my maid, but now I feel more warmly toward them. Othello and I agree that he has conciliatory skills that we can make use of. We are now off to

Cyprus, on the charge of the Duke (who looked at Othello, manly, dignified, and familiar, as you suggested, and then laughed off these charges of witchcraft). The Republic of Venice once again must engage with the Turks, and Othello is the only commander who has regular success in doing so. I am hopeful that when we return, all of these difficulties will be behind us.

Once again, I thank you for your kind and wise thoughts. Your friendship is a gift without price.

Your affectionate
Desdemona

Marguerite de Navarre to Desdemona
(sent by special messenger)

Ma chère Desdemona,

I read with alarm that you are accompanying your husband on his campaign. Please have a care in this. Your best strategy, now that you have gained your marriage and cast off the accusations of witchcraft, is to remain in your father's house until your husband's return. To do so will reinforce your reputation for virtue, and also aid you in reconciling your father's feelings to this admittedly loving, but also unorthodox marriage. Your father is no doubt smarting from two things—losing his power over you, and having this humiliation paraded in public. No one can soothe his pride more effectively that you can, ma chère fille, and right now, that is your first responsibility and greatest defense. It is the unfortunate obligation of women to soothe and, if they can, manage the pride of the men who have power over them. Please ponder this obligation! I write in haste, and send this by messenger, hoping to forestall your departure.

Your true friend,
Marguerite, Queen of Navarre

Desdemona to Marguerite de Navarre

Chère Madame,

I write to tell you that all is well here in Cyprus, although this outcome is owing to the grace of the Lord, not to our own efforts. We can have had no clearer demonstration of His powers than we have had in the last few days. Just after we left Venezia, we were overtaken by a great storm. I was much afraid, particularly because I traveled on a different ship from my husband. I did not know if my greater worry was for Othello's life or my own! But as the Lord provided, the storm abated just as we came to the harbor in Cyprus, and our ship docked safely. I was immediately taken aside by one of my husband's lieutenants, and solemnly told that nothing was known of Othello's fate. I was so struck by this that I would have fainted if he hadn't taken my hand. When my husband's ship soon docked, I must say that we were all giddy with relief. And imagine our transcendent thanks when we then understood that the Turkish ships had been broken up and lost in the storm that we had survived, thereby handing our navy the advantage. The Turks will not be back, and it looks as though these wars we have endured are over. We give the Lord our deepest thanks for His Grace. We now plan to enjoy the hospitality of Governor Montano and then return in triumph to Venezia. I send my letter in a thankful spirit, and I know, chère Madame, from your great reputation for holiness, that you will receive it in the same spirit.

Your devoted friend,
Desdemona

Marguerite de Navarre to Desdemona

Chère Desdemona,

I have indeed received your good news with gratitude, and I have offered prayers of thanks at the chapel at our seat at Mont-de-Marsan, where I am presently residing. I, too, I must say, must deal with the pride of men, and especially royal men, at every turn. My beloved brother, the King of France, goes to war every spring against his favorite enemy (and brother-in-law) Charles, the Holy Roman Emperor. These exploits are taxing in a multitude of ways, and while I understand my obligations as both a Queen and a sister, I have discovered what you will discover as you get older, that a little respite among our holy sisters is an invaluable aid to sustaining your strength of mind. On this same subject, war, I must say, with regard to your sojourn to Cyprus, it is in the nature of men who have been frustrated in their expectations of battle to be at once relieved and disappointed—they have worked themselves to a pitch of boldness in order to meet the enemy. Now the enemy has proved a chimera, but boldness still rules their hearts. They will look about for other trouble that they can get into, and this most often takes the form of disputes among themselves. Rivalries that they had set aside in order to join against the enemy must now erupt more violently. You, my dear, are also vulnerable in the society of fighting men. I do not think that one maid is much protection. You have escaped death and widowhood and war—I understand your gratitude and exhilaration. But your condition remains perilous, and I urge you to be cautious in what you say and whom you say it to. Your best course is to stay with your husband as much as possible, and otherwise keep to yourself, spurning the company of your husband's lieutenants. Whatever their intentions, their heightened spirits may damage you.

I wish you all the best.

Your distant but faithful friend,
Marguerite, Queen of Navarre

Vittoria Colonna to Marguerite de Navarre

Chère Madame Marguerite,

You will have heard through diplomatic channels of the sad events that recently took place in Turkey. To add to what you know already, I enclose two letters, one, addressed to you, that was found in Desdemona's chamber. I don't feel that they explain much. However, perhaps the events require no explanation, given what we know of the hotheaded nature of men at war and the perennial dangers that surround beautiful and innocent young women, and by innocent, I mean those young women who are both lovely and high spirited, who have courage and grace, and assume that the world is made up of well-intentioned beings such as themselves. You and I, Madame, know this to be untrue.

In sadness and love,

Your friend,
Vittoria Colonna

Enclosed: Desdemona to Marguerite de Navarre

Chère Madame—

I write in haste, and in some distress. Perhaps you will not receive this letter in time to advise me, but I do not know where else to turn. I have, I am sorry to say, told my husband a small lie. When we first declared our love for one another, he gave me an ornate handkerchief; I was to keep it with me at all times. I did so, even through the storm. But then yesterday, when he was in distress with a headache, I took it out to apply it (as you know, often binding an aching head will relieve the pain), and somehow the handkerchief was lost. I have looked everywhere for it, and my maid Emilia has done the same, but it cannot be found. Now Othello tells me that the handkerchief is a sort of oracle—its possession predicts the faithfulness or faithlessness of a spouse. I find it alarming that he might believe such a thing, but I find it more alarming that the handkerchief has simply vanished. I am both distraught and confused. I lied to my husband and said that the handkerchief was in my room, because the generous man I married has disappeared, and been replaced by an angry and suspicious stranger who stares at me but doesn't listen, quizzes me but believes nothing I say. And your predictions about disputes among the men have turned out to be correct, especially as their already strong feelings are even more heightened by the strong liquors that constitute the largest part of Governor Montana's hospitality. I— *unfinished*

Preliminary Report to the Duke of Venezia, from his Governor, Jacopo Montano

Honored Sir—

I regret to inform you of the death, by his own hand, of your esteemed general, Othello, on the island of Cyprus. While an investigation into the circumstances surrounding this appalling act is ongoing, the events are straightforward, and I did witness the suicide of said general, Othello. I am sorry to report that this suicide followed quickly on the heels of Othello's murder of his wife in a jealous rage. We do not quite understand what motivated the murder—the wife was known to be loving and faithful, and although her manner was free and high spirited, no one suspected her of any in fidelity, except, apparently, General Othello. Perhaps this may be attributed to his volatile nature, but perhaps not.

There is a young couple here, Ensign Iago and his wife, Emilia, Madame Desdemona's maid, who seem to know more than they are saying. The maid, Emilia, is in dire straits, having been stabbed by her husband, but it appears she may survive, and if so I will duly report to you her version of the events. Ensign Iago has refused to speak. I have sent him to our prison, and the customary measures are being utilized. I will report the results to you.

Marguerite de Navarre to Vittoria Colonna

Cara Madama Vittoria,

I had been wondering about and praying for the poor child Desdemona and her tormented husband. Your news of their sad fates puts our beliefs (though not our faith) once again to the test. No matter how often we come to understand that this world is merely a way station to a greater one, still we feel sorrow at the challenges our Lord poses for us. A story such as this one perplexes me. There were several ways in which the girl was foolish, but her foolishness arose from innocence and high spirits—should her punishment be so cruel? As for the husband, how is it that a man of great experience, tested in battle, with a reputation for judgment and wisdom can be so easily undone by carnal jealousy? And yet, it is something we see all the time, a perennial conundrum—how can love be both divine and debased, the source of goodness and the source of evil? You must know that, along with a few friends of mine, I am gathering together a series of tales inspired by your favorite author, Giovanni Boccaccio. My friends are much more opinionated than Signore Boccaccio's friends—they insist upon discussing every tale, and they hardly ever agree. I am offering this sad tale to them—we have already had seventy-nine tales. This will be our eightieth one. I will let you know what they say. Until that future epistle, I am

Your devoted
Marguerite, Queen of Navarre

The One and Only

Like Mozart, Charles Dickens is one of those artists whose prolific excellence defies belief, seems somehow an artifact of an earlier age when men and women had fewer conveniences and more energy, less formal education but greater literacy, shorter lives but, perhaps, longer days. His twenty novels seem to build a world at least as complex and fascinating as the world around us, and he wasn't behindhand either with stories, essays, letters, journals, children, affairs of the heart, friendships, travels and walking tours, performances, parties, and the vicissitudes of life. Anyone, like this reader, who already feels astonished and privileged to live after Dickens and thus to freely partake of the marvelous banquet that is his work, will feel no less so after perusing this new Penguin collection of his journalism.

Most lovers of English literature know that Dickens edited several magazines and that he wrote for them too, but college courses and publishers have generally focused on the novels. The editing seems like his day job—a dimly recognizable activity he must have done sometime—but in fact Dickens was a dedicated and ambitious editor who launched four magazines. *Household Words* and *All the Year Round* were successful, and Dickens was deeply involved in every aspect of their production for most of the years he was also writing novels. Indeed, his editorial opinions permeated all the pieces in both magazines. The contrast between a passage from one piece, written by Henry Morley and quoted in David Pascoe's introduction, and Dickens's revision of it, as it appeared in *Household Words*, shows not only Dickens's lively taste but also his indefatigable energy and his amazing fluency. And then he wrote a long, instructive editorial letter to Morley, which, Pascoe says, Morley was not happy to receive.

Dickens's own essays and articles slant the light into his remarkable sensibility somewhat differently than the novels do, even though, as many have pointed out, certain characters and scenes that later appeared in the novels were given dry runs in the articles. His voice, for one thing, is unabashedly personal. His great friend and correspondent, John Forster, recalled that when Dickens was casting about for a title for *Household Words*, along with *Mankind* and *Everything*, he thought of *Charles Dickens, a weekly journal designed for the instruction and entertainment of all classes of readers, Conducted by Himself.* Surely Dickens, a great wit, saw the humor in these possible titles. But the reader may also see Dickens's grand ambition as well as his own recognition of the capaciousness of his imagination.

The seventy-two pieces collected here must inevitably vary in their appeal to individual readers. As a writer and a citizen, Dickens wore many hats; the categories Pascoe has chosen emphasize that Dickens was a social critic, a political gadfly, a passionate traveler, a connoisseur of oddities, and a deeply reflective observer of his own psychology. Whether the subject is lying awake at night, crowds gathering to witness a death in Paris, an industrial strike, or governmental incompetence, all are unmistakably Dickensian—that is, all develop through the seemingly effortless accumulation of detail; all portray a complex and seething mix of the human, the mechanical, and the natural; all exhibit quick but fluid changes of mood and tone; and in all, the author's sympathies are readily apparent. Indeed, in his letter to Morley, Dickens expounded his views on the necessity of fancy, imagination, "some little grace or other" in the telling of any tale or the reporting of any incident. Of course, the outstanding hallmark of Dickens's style is his mastery of the use of figurative language—objects, processes, and people are continuously likened to other objects, processes, and people, in order to get at their underlying sense. This was both a natural habit of mind for Dickens and a conscious technique for resisting what he saw as the growing mechanization and depersonalization of the world around him. The effect is to give both intense life and intense subjectivity to every scene. For me, these pieces are not so much to be read as to be delighted in, scarfed up. Favorite passages in each give way as in music to subsequent favorite passages and finally to a feeling that Dickens's abundance defies criticism, interpretation, and even selection.

But I laugh. I laugh when he describes taking a boat to Calais:

> A stout wooden wedge driven in at my right temple and out at my left, a floating deposit of lukewarm oil in my throat, and a compression of the bridge of my nose in a blunt pair of pincers, these are the personal sensations by which I know we are off, and by which I shall continue to know it until I am on the soil of France. My symptoms have scarcely established themselves comfortably, when two or three skating shadows that have been trying to walk or stand, get flung together, and other two or three shadows in tarpaulin slide with them into corners and cover them up. Then the south foreland lights begin to hiccup at us in a way that bodes no good. [from "The Calais Night Mail"]

But I see. I see clearly that "at intervals all day, a frightened hare has shot across this whitened turf; or the distant clatter of a herd of deer trampling the hard frost, has, for the minute, crushed the silence too. Their watchful eyes beneath the fern may be shining now, if we could see them, like the icy dewdrops on the leaves, but they are still, and all is still. And so, the lights growing larger, and the trees falling back before us, and closing up again behind us, as if to forbid retreat, we come to the house" (from "A Christmas Tree").

And I hear:

Mr. Cheerful [the bookmaker], he said, had gone out on "tickler bizniz" at ten o'clock in the morning and wouldn't be back until late at night. Mrs. Cheerful was gone out of town for her health, till the winter. Would Mr. Cheerful be back tomorrow? cried the crowd. "He won't be here tomorrow," said the miraculous boy. "Coz it's Sunday, and he always goes to church, a' Sunday." At this, even the losers laughed. "Will he be here a' Monday, then?" asked a desperate young green-grocer. "A' Monday?" said the Miracle, reflecting. "No, I don't think he'll be here a' Monday, coz he's going to a sale a' Monday." [from "Betting Shops"]

I also get the point:

The power of Nobody is becoming so enormous in England, and he alone is responsible for so many proceedings, both in the way of commission and omission; he has so much to answer for, and is so constantly called to account; that a few remarks upon him may not be ill-timed.

The hand which this surprising person had in the late war is amazing to consider. It was he who left the tents behind, who left the baggage behind, who chose the worst possible ground for encampments, who provided no means of transport, who killed the horses, who paralysed the commissariat, who knew nothing of the business he professed to know and monopolized, who decimated the English army. It was Nobody who gave out the famous unroast coffee, it was Nobody who made the hospitals more horrible than language can describe, it was Nobody who occasioned all the dire confusion of Balaklava harbor, it was even Nobody who ordered the fatal Balaklava cavalry charge. The non-relief of Kars was the work of Nobody, and Nobody has justly and severely suffered for that infamous transaction. [from "Nobody, Somebody, and Everybody"]

These selected pieces are taken from the twenty years of Dickens's life that also saw the writing of all the great and massive novels after *David Copperfield*, though only one essay appeared after 1863. In June 1865, Dickens and his traveling companions were passengers on a train that crashed and went over a bridge into the River Beult, killing and injuring numerous others but leaving Dickens and his companions unharmed. It may have seemed to the author that the forces of mechanization and depersonalization had finally overwhelmed his capacity for observing and resisting them, because although he continued writing novels, he stopped writing journalistic pieces almost entirely, and those he did write had none of the verve of the earlier ones. While he escaped physically unharmed, he began, according to Pascoe, to be reluctant to write as he always had, about what he had seen. He died five years later on the anniversary of the crash.

Those of us who, unconsciously perhaps, think of Charles Dickens as more a phenomenon than a man may take special delight in *Charles Dickens: Selected Journalism 1850–1870*, for on every page his sense of himself as a particular man in a particular place and time is apparent in every sentence, and yet that ineffable other thing is there as well, that abiding inexhaustibility, that transcendent mastery of all the richnesses of the English language.

I Am Your "Prudent Amy"

When I was growing up (I think I first read *Little Women* when I was ten) I identified with Jo—she was tall, she was literary, and she represented Alcott herself. Her journey is the most prominent of the four. But now, when I look at the girls, the one I enjoy the most is Amy.

When we meet Amy on page 1, it is Christmas, and there are no presents because of the Civil War— lack of funds, frightening absence of Father. Each girl responds to the news characteristically—Jo (age 15) grumbles, Meg (16) sighs, Amy (12) offers "an injured sniff," and Beth (13 to 14) speaks last, "contentedly." The four girls then recollect that each of them has saved a bit of money, about a dollar (maybe nineteen dollars now). Meg says that she would like to buy herself some "pretty things." Jo wants a copy of a book of two fantastical stories translated from German, one about a water sprite, the other about a knight. Beth would like some music (she is the pianist), and Amy says, "decidedly," that she wants drawing pencils. None of the four seems more selfish than the others at this point, but the next passage is revealing. Each sister now issues a complaint—Meg about the children she takes care of, Jo about her "fussy" aunt, whom she also tends to, Beth about her household tasks (though she doesn't like to complain). Amy, who is the only one who goes to school, makes the most modern complaint—at twelve, she is surrounded by other twelve-year-olds. She says, "I don't believe any of you suffer as I do, for you don't have to go to school with impertinent girls, who plague you if you don't know your lessons, and laugh at your dresses, and label your father if he isn't rich, and insult you when your nose isn't nice" (by "label" Amy means "libel"). Because she negotiates the social world of what would now be junior high school, Amy is (and must be) always aware not only of her own feelings but of her social status and how she appears. In fact, Jo and Amy constitute the two types of feminists we will see in the future who will agree on some matters and disagree on others—Jo is the one who values her independence and wishes to retain it even if it leads to disagreement or unhappiness; Amy is the one who thinks that the best option for doing what she wants is to learn to navigate and make use of the world she is stuck with. We might think of Jo as the "agitator," Amy as the "political operative."

It is no surprise that of the four, Jo and Amy are the two who are most often at odds with each other. One reason is that, as every novelist knows, and as Alcott herself knew, all four of the sisters cannot be good— readers with their own daughters and sisters wouldn't buy it, and if there were no conflict, no character development, the plot would have nothing to build upon. Meg has a few faults, but she must end up as the normal wife and mother. Beth has no faults—she is the sacrificial victim (and realistically so, since many nineteenth-century children died before they reached adulthood). Jo is the central character who needs a foil, and Amy is it. If she is going to be a worthy foil, she needs to be as complex as Jo—as ready to learn, though in different ways, and as ready to do battle so that their conflict will force them to live through their learning experiences. She can't be a flat character, and she isn't—though as the youngest, most petted sister and often seen by her sisters (and by readers) as vain, calculating, and spoiled—she actually possesses the self-awareness and reflectiveness that will help her navigate her world.

Alcott was clearly inspired by John Bunyan's 1678 allegory, *The Pilgrim's Progress*—the evidence is in her epigraph—but her subjects were modern girls living in the modern world. Their job is to negotiate real events—war, poverty, family life, career aspirations, and, of course, growing into womanhood. But what is their goal? Marmee would say that it is to be kind, self-sacrificing, womanly, generous; to marry, have children, and serve others; and indeed they do, when they get to the Hummels' shack: Hannah builds the fire, Marmee tends to the mother and baby, and Meg, Jo, Beth, and Amy (who has offered to "'take the cream and the muffins,' . . . heroically giving up the article she most liked") lay out the provisions and feed the hungry children. Their Christmas is merry and their lesson is a religious one, as Meg understands: the lesson of loving thy neighbor.

Alcott's theory of child development is specifically Christian, as were most American theories of child development until the early twentieth century. Marmee's goal is to get Meg, Jo, Beth, and Amy to adhere to a set of general principles. She chooses to do it through kind persuasion rather than force, and the two volumes of *Little Women* constitute a demonstration of how that system works. Marmee's job is not the one most modern American mothers take on: to investigate the individuality of her children, to contemplate their differences and decide whether their qualities are a product of nature or nurture. It never occurs to Marmee to wonder whether the chaos of having four daughters in six years, and in moderate circumstances, has caused those daughters to develop in idiosyncratic ways. As a mother, I would have told her that Amy was certainly shaped, and in some ways benefited, by the inevitable neglect she would have experienced as a baby and a toddler when her sisters were five, four, and two—she would have had plenty of time on her own to explore her world and think her own thoughts. Those of us with several children know that she would also have had to avoid being bullied, to protect her toys and her other possessions from the older girls, and to assert herself from time to time.

Alcott herself was from an interesting family that had strong convictions—her uncle, Samuel J. May, was minister of the Unitarian church in Brooklyn, Connecticut (who gave the first women's rights sermon in the US), and her mother, Abigail May, met Bronson Alcott when she was visiting her uncle. Abigail and Bronson married on May 23, 1830, and had their first two daughters within the next two and a half years. The Unitarians were known for their promotion of temperance, women's rights, and the abolition of slavery. Bronson Alcott was famous (or infamous) for educational ideas that would now seem progressive—class discussions of hot-button issues, such as the meaning of biblical stories, or having students explore their own experiences through writing about them. His forays into teaching or starting progressive schools garnered significant criticism and no money. Around the time that May Alcott (the model for Amy) was born, the family was living in Concord, Massachusetts, and being supported by Ralph Waldo Emerson. When Louisa was ten, Bronson bought some property and attempted to set up an ideal community—no meat, no animal labor, no leather or fabrics that were grown by means of slave labor (cotton, silk, wool). The experiment lasted seven months. This family background had a strong influence on Louisa. She herself later said that she had a powerful religious experience (though she never officially joined a church): "running in the Concord woods early one fall morning, she stopped to see the sunshine over the meadows. 'A very strange and solemn feeling came over me as I stood there,' she wrote in her journal, 'with no sound but the rustle of the pines, no one near me, and the sun so glorious, as for me alone. It seemed as if I felt God as I never did before, and I prayed in my heart that I might keep that happy sense of nearness all my life.'"

When a publisher suggested that she write a book for girls, she realized that as an unmarried woman with no children, she didn't particularly like girls, so she turned to her own experiences for material. When she sat down to write *Little Women*, she recalled the precepts that her mother had employed to raise her and her sisters while contending with the chaos produced by her principled and eccentric father, and she also pulled from the actual lives of herself and her three sisters. By the time Louisa was writing *Little Women*, May was in her mid-twenties, and had spent much of her life learning to teach children or teaching them. She was an active artist, studied when she was in her late teens at the School of the Museum of Fine Arts in Boston, and also supplied the illustrations for *Little Women*, as well as publishing her own art book, called *Concord Sketches*. Like Louisa, she was single, and she remained single until she was in her late thirties.

•

Perhaps the first in-depth exploration of Amy's experiences, and also the first hurdle Amy experiences in her path to self-knowledge, is in chapter 7. In order to claim some status at her school, Amy thinks she must share with the other girls a treat that is the latest craze, pickled limes (which are actually lime wedges preserved in salt). Meg gives her a quarter, worth maybe five dollars today; Amy buys some pickled limes and carries them to school in a brown paper bag. Then comes a classic episode of bullying that every modern girl can recognize—she gets some praise from her teacher for maps she has drawn, and the girl who envies the praise tattletales to the teacher about the pickled limes. Amy is called to the front of the room, forced to throw the limes out the window, then subjected to having her hand smacked with a ruler. The pain is not as great as the humiliation, and, perhaps thinking of Bronson Alcott's educational principles, Alcott writes, "During the twelve years of her life, she had been governed by love alone, and a blow of that sort had never touched her." Since physical punishment, sometimes brutal, was routine in the nineteenth century (and stories from my own relatives born in the 1880s and '90s attest to this), this line is perhaps the most radical in the book so far—I don't think most of us in the twenty-first century understand how routine whipping and humiliation were to nineteenth-century educational theories. Marmee "comforts" Amy by criticizing her: "You are getting to be altogether too conceited and important, my dear, and it is quite time you set about correcting it. You have a good many little gifts and virtues, but there is no need of parading them, for conceit spoils the finest genius." This lesson is then demonstrated when Laurie, who is playing chess with Jo, praises Beth's musical talent and Beth is too modest to realize he is talking about her. It is true that Amy took the pickled limes to school in order to elevate her status. But it was showing off by giving gifts, not by preening or bragging. I, perhaps, am more forgiving than Marmee is. Amy then voices the lesson she has learned from the events in her chapter: "I see, it's nice to have accomplishments, and be elegant, but not to show off, or get perked up." Even so, I'm not going to condemn her.

What would I, a twentieth- and twenty-first-century mother, have done and said in similar circumstances? In the first place, Marmee never addresses the real crime, which was the envious reporting of the limes by the other student. She seems to believe that bullying and backstabbing is so much the norm that the only thing a bullied child can do is turn the other cheek. Jo does take a letter to the school and Amy does leave, but Marmee never talks to Amy about the injustice, except to suggest that maybe she deserved it. When my own children were bullied in school, I went to the teachers and the principal, and they attempted to rein in the bullies, not the bullied. In addition, considering that when I was about Amy's age, my eighth-grade history teacher wrote on my report card, "She only does what she wants to do," thinking that was a bad thing, I would also have told Marmee that focus, desire, determination, and resistance, qualities that Amy has, are what lead to accomplishment and self-realization.

We are now just under a third of the way into the novel, but even though Jo is the principal character, we have seen enough of Amy to understand that she has potential that others, even Marmee, don't perceive.

The next person to hurt Amy's feelings is Jo, who, Amy discovers, is planning to go with Meg and Laurie to a play at a nearby theater. Amy knows of the show and wants to accompany the others, but the older girls don't simply tell her that there aren't enough tickets or that the seats have already been reserved; they instead disdain her—Jo says, "Little girls shouldn't ask questions," and Meg, though speaking more kindly, says, "Be a good child." Amy is enraged and calls out, "You'll be sorry for this, Jo March, see if you ain't." Everything seems fine when they get home; Jo checks her things because Amy has a history of vengeful acts, and the previous argument had ended in Amy pulling out the top drawer of Jo's dresser and upending it. Alcott writes that both girls have "quick tempers." What Amy has done this time is much more serious, though—she has burned the manuscript Jo has been working on. After confessing, she shows no immediate remorse, and Jo grabs her and shakes her "till her teeth chattered in her head." Amy then attempts to apologize, but her apology is rejected. Marmee stays out of it, knowing that Jo has to back away from her anger on her own. (If I had discovered that one of my children shook the other until her teeth chattered, I would have NOT stayed out of it.) The next day, Jo and Laurie leave Amy behind once again, when they go skating on the nearby river. Amy wants to go along and Meg advises her to do so, thinking that Laurie and the exercise will put Jo in a better mood. When Amy follows them to the river, Jo ignores her. Because Amy is not very near the older kids and is concentrating on getting going, she doesn't hear Laurie warn about the fragile ice away from the banks. The worst thing that Jo does is ignore her own conscience, thinking, "No matter whether she heard or not, let her take care of herself." Jo's punishment is instantaneous: the ice breaks, and Amy falls through into "the black water." It is Laurie who saves Amy, with Jo's help. After they get Amy home and she is safe in bed, Alcott devotes the rest of the chapter to Jo's conversation with Marmee about what Marmee has learned about rectifying her faults and errors, and what Jo needs to learn about controlling her temper. Jo swears she will make her best effort, but what seems to be overlooked is not only Amy's pain and fear but also that Amy never again acts out of rage or thoughtlessness—as usual, she learns her lesson on her own, and the lesson is that if anyone is going to take care of her, it must be herself.

A few pages later, Marmee details her hopes and dreams for her daughters to Meg and Jo—she wants them "to be beautiful, accomplished, and good; to be admired, loved, and respected." In other words, the first thing she wants—or the first thing she thinks of—is that she wants them to be seen by others in a positive way, to achieve social standing in a physical way, an intellectual way, and a moral way, in that order. Meg and Jo then draw her out, and the conversation turns to marriage—should it be for money, or not for money? All three of them recognize that a nineteenth-century woman's economic comfort is not often in her own hands, that most women have to marry to support themselves; and Marmee is very specific when she says, "I'd rather see you poor men's wives, if you were happy, beloved, contented, than queens on thrones, without self-respect or peace." It is Jo who voices Alcott's own choice—"Then we'll be old maids." Someone has to. Meg is destined by her author to be the happy, beloved, and contented poor man's wife, so Jo and Amy must decide who is to be the old maid, and who the rich man's wife.

I do not remember receiving any advice from my mother, or giving any advice to my daughters, about overarching goals—what I wanted was for them to have goals of their own, and the way they were to discover them was through education. My mother read my report cards, made sure I did my homework, went to teacher–parent conferences, encouraged reading and going to the library; I did the same with my daughters. The path to womanhood was through the corridors at school and on the playground, where we learned to socialize with the other students and navigate the larger world. I thought that my job as a mother was not to think of beauty first, or even admiration; it was to think of effort, of proper behavior, of thought, of ambition. My job as a girl was to look around and decide what I wanted to do, what I was able to do, and how these two things might be combined. I did not think about my children growing up to be "good"—I knew that if they were good now, they would be good as adults. I would not have taken Amy out of her school, or if I had, I would have found her another. Once she is removed from the school, her growing understanding of the social world must become more random, less productive. But she keeps at it because she is smart enough to understand that she has to in order to grow up and also to get what she wants.

In this way, too, Amy is more modern than her sisters. She goes about shaping her life in a conscious manner that seems calculated to the other girls. For example, as *Little Women* unfolds, a lot of attention is given to Jo's literary efforts, because whatever they are, and Jo herself admits they are trashy, they help support the family. Amy is as just as dedicated to her own artistic efforts—in chapter 4, Alcott writes that her sisters call her "Little Raphael" and that she has "a decided talent for drawing and was never so happy as when copying flowers, designing fairies, or illustrating stories with queer specimens of art." Let's say that if I were her mother, I would not say "queer"—I would say "original"—but as time passes, her efforts come to be seen by the other members of her family as a demonstration of vanity, partly because she would rather make "mud pies" than do housework. Her taste improves—she moves on from mud pies to drawing, "poker art," and painting. But the family needs money, and Jo's popular magazine stories do make some, while Amy's efforts make none. The mud pies reveal something about Amy, even though the words are a bit derogative—she knows that in order to learn, she has to make do with materials that the family can afford. The others might be amused at her efforts, but she knows what any artist would tell her—that practice of any kind is productive. Once again a modern woman in the making, she wants to find a way to express herself. We can compare her efforts to Jo's literary ones—Jo writes her pulp fiction tales without thinking about whether she is expressing her own inner life. Because Amy is learning, and not earning money, she is focused on developing her vision and her skills.

•

When the girls' father is injured in the Civil War, and Marmee and Mr. Brooke must go to him, leaving the girls in the care of Hannah, the girls discuss how they will handle their unease. Jo says, "Hope and keep busy is the motto for us." Meg is vexed about having to go to her child-care job; she would rather help around the house. Amy "with an important air" declares that she, Beth, and Hannah can take care of the house, and then, taking a bit of sugar, she adds what I consider to be one of her most revealing remarks, "I think anxiety is very interesting." The other girls can't help laughing in response. But what Amy is showing is a penchant for introspection, for weighing all aspects of her temperament—her feelings, her desires, her needs, her obligations—and sorting them out so that she can learn from them. As a youngest child who must observe her three older sisters, as well as Marmee, Hannah, and her other relatives, she has a large amount of data to sort through—youngest children may be dismissed, but they cannot dismiss. They are forced to contemplate the psychology of the others—what works, what doesn't work, what they can or cannot get away with, and how they might push that envelope subtly and effectively. Amy already knows that bribery—that is, pickled limes—doesn't work. As she grows up, she recognizes that what does work is a combination of charm, determination, and self-knowledge. These qualities are demonstrated in her letter to Marmee in chapter 16. Alcott makes fun of her a bit by including her misspellings and vanities (one of which is signing a letter to her own mother with her formal name, "Amy Curtis March"), but as silly as the letter is intended to be (she writes, "Meg says my punchtuation and spelling are disgraceful and I am mortyfied but dear me I have so many things to do, I can't stop"), it is clear even in its single paragraph that Amy is interested in behaving properly, feeling calm and comforted, having an indulgence or two, not being teased (by Laurie), dressing correctly, taming her own feelings of dissatisfaction, organizing her activities, and expressing love for her parents. Amy is the one who comes to understand that anxiety can be enlightening if she is willing to examine its sources.

When Beth starts to come down with scarlet fever, Amy happens not to be nearby. Meg and Jo agree to take care of Beth, and Amy, because she hasn't had scarlet fever, is sent away, over her objections, to Aunt March, their father's wealthy aunt. At first Amy is lonely and resentful—she realizes "how much she was beloved and petted at home." Jo had been tending to Aunt March as a way of earning some money, but did not get along with her and was resentful of Aunt March's rules and crotchets. Amy begins with the same attitude, but in fact, Aunt March likes Amy because she is "more docile and amiable" than Jo. I would say that Amy's behavior is not so much docile and amiable—those words imply that Amy dissembles in order to get along with her great-aunt—as it is thoughtful and reserved, owing to her desire to learn from her new surroundings. She is now being exposed to a different, more elegant culture than the one she knows at home, in part because Aunt March has money, but also through Esther, Aunt March's French maid. Esther not only tells Amy about France, Catholicism, and her own upbringing but also shows her Aunt March's treasures: her diamonds, her pearls, and her turquoise ring, which is the one Amy likes the most. Esther, in the true Balzac tradition, reveals to Amy that she has witnessed Aunt March's will, and knows that the jewels are going to the March sisters after she dies. When, as a result of this, Amy becomes the "docile and amiable" attendant Aunt March desires, her new behavior is morally complex—Jo's resistance to her aunt, by comparison, is presented as an honorable assertion that her aunt can't buy her off. But if Amy were my daughter, forced to live with a disagreeable relative because of a family crisis, I would advise her to find ways to get along, to try to understand the complexities of the difficult relative's psychology, to please the relative as a way of making the relative not only more agreeable but happier. Family conflict is not merely a financial issue. If there really was an Aunt March in the Alcott family, perhaps it was she who was offended by Bronson Alcott's peculiarities, and what she longed for was a relative she could like and care for. Amy is a realist who thinks the ring is beautiful, and she would like to have it; her artistic endeavors show that she is attracted and moved by beauty, but she also knows that what she is learning by living with Aunt March and Esther is worthwhile because her sense of the world is being expanded and enriched.

Amy again internalizes her lesson, this time by writing her own will, which the others go along with as if it were a pleasant joke. But the will is a sign of Amy's constantly growing understanding of how the world works—she knows, because of her father's illness, the Hummel baby's death, and Beth's illness, that death is a constant threat that can strike suddenly. She knows that she has possessions that she values and that she wishes for her relatives to value, and she knows that being thoughtful and organized is the best option. When she decides how she is going to distribute her legacy, she also takes a stab at understanding the desires of her friends and relatives and leaves them, along with other things, what she thinks they would most desire. When she is discussing the will with Laurie, who is evidently humoring her, she adds what she calls "a postscript," though Laurie corrects her, telling her it is a "codicil." After she dies, she would like to have her hair cut and locks given to everyone—she not only knows that her hair, thick, curly, and golden, is her glory but also knows that she would like to be remembered as a person, not merely as a producer of art. Her will shows that Amy has the wisdom and self-knowledge to plan for the possibility of death. Then, when Laurie tells her that Beth is still in serious condition, she secretly goes into the chapel she and Esther have built, and prays, with tears, for Beth's recovery, demonstrating that she has plenty of feelings that she is wary of revealing, unlike Jo, who habitually acts on impulse.

The day Marmee comes home, Beth recovers from her bout of scarlet fever, and Laurie is sent to Aunt March's house to tell Amy the good news. Amy's first thought is that her private prayers have paid off. Marmee appears, and Amy takes her to her private "chapel" and explains how she has been making use of it. For once Marmee is approving, but her approval only lasts until she sees the turquoise ring that Aunt March has given her. She says, "I think you're rather young for such ornaments, Amy." By this time, perhaps because of those hours of introspection the chapel represents, Amy has enough self-knowledge to respond that the ring is not a display but a reminder to not be selfish. Marmee is amused, though she hides her amusement. But what Amy says to her mother demonstrates that the arc of her particular plot has been accomplished. It is not exactly that she has learned not to be vain or selfish but that she has figured out a way to coordinate all of her ambitions. The ring symbolizes not only what she knows but also what she wants and how she can go about getting it. She understands that investigating her feelings and molding her fears and desires in private (the chapel) can lead to understanding and getting along with others, including others who are wealthy and powerful, namely Aunt March and Laurie.

How she contrasts to Jo in this is evident in the next requirement of the plot, which is getting Meg married off to Laurie's tutor, John Brooke. Amy plays no part in the brouhaha between Aunt March and Meg that causes Meg to realize that she does love John and does wish to marry him (Aunt March is offended that Meg refuses to marry for money), but Amy's final observation demonstrates her way of looking at things: "'You can't say "nothing pleasant ever happens now," can you, Meg?' said Amy, trying to decide how she would group the lovers in the sketch she was planning to make." Her role is to observe, to weigh one event against the other, to figure out how to represent the events and the feelings in her chosen art form in a way that will make sense of them both for herself and for others. By the end of volume 1, Meg has learned to love, Jo has learned to accept that her impulsive desires can't always be fulfilled, Beth has learned to survive. Amy is now thirteen, and if she were my daughter, I would say that her mind works in a sophisticated way—she has learned the most subtle and perhaps the most important lesson—to pay attention, both to herself and to others.

•

Volume 2 begins three years later, when Meg is old enough to get married. In volume 2, Amy is no longer made fun of or ignored by her author. She is sixteen. Jo is now earning some money with her writing; Laurie has gone to college and has an active social life among the local privileged young men. Alcott is straightforward about how Amy's response to Laurie's friends differs from Jo's—Jo feels so much like one of them that it seems natural to her to behave as they do. They like her, but "never fell in love with her." A few of them give Amy the sort of attention that young men of social standing in the nineteenth century accorded to attractive but well-protected young women, "paying the tribute of a sentimental sigh or two at Amy's shrine." Her role is to be appealing but remote, to lure them with her looks and behavior but never allow them to think she can be claimed. A signal of her power is that she "dared to order them about," which surprises Beth. The only things that give her this power, since the March family has very little money or social standing, are her self-possession, her looks, and her choice to be assertive.

In some ways, the central character of volume 2 is Laurie. Now that he is out of school and launched into the social world of wealth, he is in danger of wasting his time, wasting his money, or becoming dissolute. Throughout the two volumes, he has many good qualities—he is generous, affectionate, kind, exuberant, and willing to learn (though sometimes he has to be prodded to do so). His main problem is that he has no sense of purpose, unlike every one of the March girls. Alcott implies that this is the effect of too much money, but also the effect of losing his own parents, and therefore having no strong models of respectable choices. School does not give him a goal or a mission, and there are no passages in the novel about how Laurie experiences his schooling other than as a way to connect with other young men of his social class; college is more of a club than a library. His grandfather is not really in a position to save him, so his redemption falls to the Marches. Alcott's somewhat implausible narrative task is to keep him in the family, because he is a main character in the novel and is charming—to marry him off to some random girl would mean that this young woman would have to be incorporated into a group of young women we know very well. Would she be a source of conflict or estrangement? Would she have her own point of view, her own issues that would cause plot twists or digressions? If she did not join the family in a believable way, then Laurie would have to be abandoned as a principal character. But whom must he marry to stay in the family?

It cannot be Meg, because her marriage must demonstrate Marmee's thoughts about how ideal marriages work.

It cannot be Beth, because (1) she is too sickly to take on marital responsibilities, and (2) she must die.

Readers of volume 1—and there were lots of them, since it was a huge success—wanted Laurie to marry Jo, but Alcott herself was not married, and did not want the character she based on herself to betray her own sense of independence, so the only one left was Amy, and Alcott's narrative task was to make this marriage not only believable but interesting.

The fact that Amy has developed into "the flower of the family" does not prevent her from having something of the same sort of humiliating experience in the third chapter of part 2 that she had in part 1 when she took the pickled limes to school. She has been diligently working on her art, and has been taking a drawing class with some other girls. At the end of the semester (as we would call it), she decides to invite the other girls to a "fete" so elaborately planned that Jo, hard at work on her novel, is annoyed. She exclaims, "Why in the world should you spend your money, worry your family, and turn the house upside down for a parcel of girls who don't care a sixpence for you?" And in fact the fete does go wrong—only one of the girls shows up, but Amy and her family entertain her, and she has a good time in the end. Jo's response to the failure of Amy's plans is to laugh, Marmee's is to regret Amy's disappointment, but this time, Amy is not disappointed—she says, "I am satisfied; I've done what I undertook, and it's not my fault that it failed." And she seems to have learned the same thing with regard to her strenuous artistic endeavors, described earlier in the chapter—she has made use of the materials at hand, including hand-me-down paints and palettes and local scenery; she has taught herself to keep trying—slow and steady, the tortoise rather than the hare. Could Amy, too, make money from her work and help support the family? Jo is the model when she takes up popular fiction. It is possible that Amy could illustrate books or draw cartoons for newspapers. But once again, Amy's job as a character is to contrast with Jo, if only because the reader would turn away if both characters made the same choices, had the same ambitions. As a "political operative" rather than an "agitator," Amy aims with her art to express her individuality, but also to make use of the system, not wreck it.

In the sixth chapter of the second book, Amy begins organizing Jo, something I have seen younger siblings do, and usually in the reasonable manner that a smaller and weaker person must adopt. Meg has attempted to do it by example, Marmee with good advice, Beth by sweetness, and Aunt March with impatience and sharp reproaches, but Jo continues to be outspoken, impulsive, and not especially feminine. Amy knows that social interaction is worthwhile and productive; she pushes Jo to fulfill a bargain she has made to accompany Amy on "half a dozen calls," in return for a sketch Amy made of Beth. Amy understands, as she did about the fete, that being well connected is valuable, whether or not all of the connections are pleasant. (Perhaps this is the lesson she learned from having to put up with Aunt March as well as from going to school.) She also knows that Jo needs practice repaying her end of the bargain. Amy's method of reforming Jo is debate—Jo uses several arguments in an attempt to weasel out of the calls; Amy's response sounds like one a mother or an older sister might make, telling Jo how to dress, how to behave, and why they are making this effort, but doing so with much patience and some flattery, keeping at it until Jo has been guided to the first call. Jo, of course, uses the first call to make fun of Amy's assertions—she adopts a stylish demeanor but doesn't say anything, leading the woman they have called on, Mrs. Chester, to declare that she is "haughty" and "uninteresting"— the sisters overhear her remark as they leave the house.

(Jo has caused annoyance, as agitators do.) But Amy keeps at it in spite of her own feelings of disappointment. The first benefit of their day of visits is that they have a long conversation as they walk from house to house, making progress in their understanding of each other, and the second, as it turns out, is that no matter how hard she tries, Amy cannot make Jo understand how to be agreeable, and so Amy unexpectedly profits by her contrast with her sister. Their last visit is to Aunt March and Aunt Carroll, who are discussing something that they set aside when the girls appear. We hear the hint about what they are discussing when the two women ask Jo and Amy about their language skills. Jo says that she is "very stupid about studying languages" and that she "can't bear French, it's such a slippery, silly sort of language." Amy says that she has learned a lot of French from Esther, Aunt March's French maid, and that she is grateful for it. The die is cast.

As the only one of the girls whose job will be to navigate the social world, Amy's challenges have to grow larger and more complex. Having impressed Mrs. Chester during their social visit, she is invited to be part of a "fair," an event where various tables are set up and manned by well-dressed, socially prominent young women of about Amy's age. Amy begins at one of the prominent tables, but is suddenly and unaccountably moved to the flower table, on the periphery. The first day doesn't go well and Amy is disheartened, but when Marmee, Jo, and Laurie find out what has happened,

Laurie comes to the rescue by having his gardener sup-
ply her the second day with "a wilderness of flowers."
The March family and Laurie and his friends surround
her table, buy the flowers, and make her spot the liveliest
at the fair and the most profitable. Jo not only amuses
people visiting the table but also walks around, scouting
for information, and discovers that May Chester, Mrs.
Chester's daughter, about Amy's age, had betrayed her
because she was jealous that Amy's table had been a
prominent one. May apologizes, apparently sincerely,
and then Laurie's friends go to her table and buy her
goods, too. The result is not departure, as when Amy
leaves the school after the limes incident, or quiet acceptance, as when Amy acknowledges the failure of her
fete by being satisfied that she at least did her job, but
general reconciliation, pleasure, and success. Amy has
learned to navigate the specifically female social world
by making the best of her assigned place, but also by
enlisting allies and putting on a good face. She ends up
not only being accepted but having an enjoyable day.
The other girls all praise her; Marmee says nothing,
and if I had been in the room, I wouldn't have said anything either—Amy's lesson has been learned by all of
them. And then Aunt Carroll sends a letter, inviting her
along on a trip to Europe.

Jo and Amy now have to work out whatever conflicts or jealousy Jo feels about Amy's fulfillment of a
wish that Jo has also had for a long time. When she
first finds out about the invitation, Jo asserts that Amy

will have "all the fun." Amy tells Jo what she hopes to do—to practice her art and find out, once and for all, whether she has any "genius"—she is looking for inspiration and to understand herself, and she plans to work hard at it. Like a modern young woman embarking on an independent life, she is also thinking about her other options, as she always does, as she has learned to do—if she has no genius, she is well aware that she can become an art teacher, or she can marry a wealthy man and fund artists who do have genius. Alcott uses their conversation to illustrate Amy's and Jo's different but also reasonable approaches to making their lives. The conversation goes directly to one of the major differences between them—money. Jo is the one who writes popular fiction for money; Amy is the one who scrapes together what materials she can find to pursue her artistic ambitions and makes no money, as yet. Jo's moneymaking is seen as a necessity so that the Marches can get by. Because Amy dresses well, behaves properly, and gets along with Aunt March, she is the one whose character is a bit clouded for many readers by Amy's understanding that marrying for money is an option. By this point in volume 2, Amy has made good arguments about the value of reason, understanding, thoughtfulness, getting along. Amy is not more selfish than Jo—she is more canny. If we return to the spot in volume 1 where Marmee tells Meg and Jo what she wants for her daughters, the first descriptive word out of her mouth is "beautiful." It is Amy who has done what her mother wanted, who has used her looks—that is, become beautiful in the eyes of the society—to get ahead, but she has done so not out of vanity or greed but because, through her art, she has sought to understand the nature of beauty.

Once she departs on her trip, even though Amy is accompanied by her aunt, her uncle, and her cousin Flo (who seems to be about Amy's age), Amy is on her own in a way she has never been before—even on the ship, she is healthy and active, exploring the decks and the views, while "Aunt and Flo were poorly all the way." In the first letter she sends home, she remarks, "Gentlemen really are very necessary on board a ship, it's a mercy to make them useful, to hold on to, or to wait upon one; and as they have nothing to do, otherwise they would smoke themselves to death, I'm afraid." Amy's trip is a whirlwind tour of what it means to be worldly, and she makes use of the opportunity. In general, her letters are amusing and high spirited. She becomes involved in a practice romance, with one of Laurie's English friends, Fred Vaughn, but she understands that although Fred is strongly attracted to her, he is "rash," while she is "prudent" (well aware of all the lessons she has learned).

In the meantime, Jo gets away too, though not as far as Europe. Alcott's principal task for the rest of volume 2 is to marry off Jo and Amy, and to do so in a way that her readers will accept and that illustrates her theories about love, marriage, and money. I remember when I was reading *Little Women* as a girl, I sensed as soon as he entered that Professor Bhaer was to claim Jo, and I was put off—he was too old, too exotic. Reading it as an adult, I understand his appeal to Jo—he is witty and good-natured, easygoing, apparently able to calm her and advise her. Laurie, the handsome, youthful, energetic, talented, wayward young man charges Jo up, triggers her pleasure in conflict, as is evident in the chapter, "Heartache," when he proposes to her, over her own objections, and is argumentatively rejected. We all knew this was coming, but it is a sign of his passion that even though he knew it too, he's willing to try. What attracts him is their long relationship, Jo's enterprise and feistiness. After she turns Laurie down, it is not unbelievable that Mr. Laurence might take him to Europe—Mr. Laurence has been the example of a wealthy American cosmopolitan all along. The difficult task is to get Amy and Laurie together in a believable and sympathetic manner, and Alcott begins by portraying the freshly minted grown-up Amy whom Laurie encounters in Nice:

> As she stood at the distant window with her head half turned and one hand gathering up her dress, the slender, white figure against the red curtains was as effective as a well-placed statue.

Amy is not attempting to woo Laurie—she is attempting to show him that the girl he thought he knew is now a woman who both fits in in Europe and does not—she continues to possess certain American traits, such as a love of physical activity, which she shows when they go to a ball, and she "neither romped nor sauntered, but danced with spirit and grace, making the delightsome pastime what it should be." She doesn't dance with Laurie at first, but does something more effective—lets him watch her and gauge her qualities from a distance as she dances with other men. Then she sits with him and demonstrates her new self-knowledge when they have a straightforward and amusing conversation. In other words, they are made for each other—they can operate in society and enjoy themselves in the presence of others (because unlike Jo, Amy minds her manners), but they can also have an honest connection in which Amy, unlike many women of her era, can speak and be heard, not in spite of her poverty, but because she has learned how to make the most of that very poverty—in chapter 14, she is honest about how she put together the old dress, the tulle, and the posies (flowers), "making the most of my poor little things." Laurie then monopolizes her for the rest of the evening.

Alcott is clear that Amy has not set her cap for Laurie, nor is she attempting to entrap him. After an interlude with Meg and John, we go back to Nice and observe how their relationship develops. They spend a lot of time together, and the more time they spend, the more Laurie is impressed, but Amy is not—she comes to have the same opinion of him that Jo and his grandfather have, that he is idling his youth away, has no purpose in life, always takes the easy way out. They go for a ride and then a walk, and she does again what she tried to do with Jo—to use reasoned argument to convince him to do what he should: to visit his grandfather and thereby meet his obligations. She makes use of her talent for conversation and banter (even telling him "I despise you") to keep Laurie talking until he hears her true opinion, "Because with every chance to be good, useful, and happy, you are faulty, lazy, and miserable." He knows, having observed her for a month, that Amy herself is the example of someone who has chosen to make use of her chances to be good, useful, and happy, that she has put up with him and not pushed him away, as Jo did; and her "calm, cool voice" is more convincing than the impatience of others who have tried to reform him. And patience isn't her only weapon. Sometime later, he looks at a sketch she has made of him lying in the grass. He sees his own idleness, but he also sees her artistic skill, and admires the way that her hard work has borne fruit. When he goes off to make use of his time and opportunities, she says she is glad he is gone, but she knows, maybe not as well as the reader knows, that she "will miss him." Her attempt to argue Jo into reforming did not work, but her attempt with Laurie does.

After Beth's death, the question is not whether Amy and Laurie will marry—the reader already expects them to—but how they will get there, so Alcott delves into their inner lives as they go about their business. Amy turns down Fred Vaughn, not angrily, but decidedly; Laurie tries pursuing art and music; when he composes an opera, he wants Jo to be the female lead, but he can't put her in—she is too unappealing. He puts someone in, and that someone turns out, he realizes, to be based on his thoughts and feelings about Amy. She sends him pleasant letters and sketches, and vows to be agreeable. Because the two are traveling, the letters about Beth's illness never reach them, and when they separately get the news of her death, they rush to find each other. When Amy sees Laurie, she understands their shared grief and his kindness, generosity, and love in coming from Germany to Switzerland to comfort her (and himself). In this way, Alcott defines their love as specifically theirs, made up of their psychological quirks and predispositions (let's say "nature" and "nurture," or "temperament" and "history"), and in contrast to the love Meg and John share, and the love Jo and Professor Bhaer share.

Jo accepts Professor Bhaer. (They later go on to establish a progressive school rather like the schools that Alcott's father, Bronson, was known for.) Jo must evolve, too, and she does, especially after she meets Bhaer and understands that he offers her an opportunity that she never thought she would have—to feel love. Laurie and Jo realize they are better as friends and as brother and sister than they might have been as husband and wife—another form of love—and Amy accepts that she might not have realized all her artistic ambitions, but she loves her life, her husband, and her frail baby daughter named after Beth ("the dread of losing her was the shadow over Amy's sunshine"). Self-aware to the end, Amy tells her mother what she has learned. Yes, Amy is the one to achieve the classic happy ending—true love, ideal mate, plenty of money, happiness—but from the beginning to the end of *Little Women*, Alcott has made sure that the reader knows that such an ending was earned through constant self-awareness and observation.

And here is the poignant postscript—May Alcott did make her name in the art world—a painting of hers, *La Negresse*, was exhibited at the 1879 Paris Salon, the most prestigious show in France or, some say, in the world at the time. Her painting was the only one by an American woman artist in the exhibition. And she did have a daughter, whom she gave birth to at the age of thirty-nine. But she died when the baby was seven weeks old, and for the next eight years, Louisa raised her until she herself died at the age of fifty-four.

Because of the tremendous popularity of *Little Women*, readers continue to contemplate the sisters. If Amy were my child, I would be proud of her—that she worked hard and sorted herself out in a methodical and productive way—and pleased with her, because she understands that pleasing others while continuing to adhere to her own goals is a good way to make peace in the family and in the social world. There are many women characters in novels (and women in life) who are thoughtful, cautious, observant, intelligent, and ambitious. Quite often, the words used to describe them are "cold, calculating, money hungry, shallow, and social-climbing." The task that Alcott knows she must complete with Amy, and that she accomplishes, is integrating Amy's inner life and her appearance so that the reader sees the complexity and subtleties of how she starts out and how she forms herself. In some ways, this is more of a challenge than portraying the characters of Meg, Jo, and Beth. It is evident as volume 2 progresses and Alcott gives more time to Amy, especially to her self-expression, that she enjoys the challenge. Amy is the modern woman, the thoughtful feminist, the sister, who stays true to herself, learns to navigate her social world, and gains a wisdom and self-knowledge different from her sisters' and more like what we aim for.

Why Go On?

Not long ago, I read a novel that Anthony Trollope wrote around the time of his sixty-fourth birthday. It took him about five weeks, and runs about 225 pages. It came in at number forty-four out of his forty-seven published novels. Trollope also wrote plenty in plenty of other forms—notably travel and biography. When he died at sixty-seven, in 1882, he had been publishing for thirty-five years, much of that time also working for the English post office. As it happens, my work has been on the market for forty years now. I've published thirty-one books. I do not think I can produce fourteen more. But Trollope and other vastly prolific authors fascinate me. Although in some ways, writers who write "too much" are demeaned by the critics, and even by readers, I'm not exactly interested in how they are received—what interests me is how their minds work, what it is that draws them on when they have been, perhaps, as successful as they can hope to be. I am interested, too, in what draws me on. Perhaps it ought to be the money, but it isn't.

The novel I read, *Doctor Wortle's School*, concerns the proprietor of a fashionable and successful school for the sons of wealthy English aristocrats. As the novel opens, Dr. Wortle discovers that he has hired a couple to work at the school who are not actually married. Trollope reveals the mystery about the couple at once in order to focus on his protagonist's dilemma, one that is simultaneously moral, temperamental, and economic. (A mother he has already done battle with and vanquished is likely to hear about the scandal and use it to destroy the school.) Trollope is clear that Dr. Wortle has brought these dangers upon himself—he is headstrong and hot tempered. He proudly goes his own way and asserts himself vigorously against even the most minor efforts on the part of his superiors to control him. He is, in many respects, the closest Trollope ever came to a self-portrait.

Though I have always loved Dickens, I find myself pondering Trollope, who was more prolific, more physically active, better traveled, and in some ways more experimental than his legendary rival. Dickens died at fifty-seven, hugely successful but somewhat (I would say) bogged down in his last novel, a murder mystery whose solution seems not quite mysterious enough. No one ever asks why Dickens kept at it—in addition to his having to support several expensive households and maintaining at least three separate existences, there is something in the novels themselves that seems driven, almost hallucinatory—he kept at it because he was nuts.

But Trollope is careful to show in his autobiography that he is not nuts—in a remarkable paragraph that comes right after a list of his novels and how much money (down to the penny) he made from each, he writes, "To enjoy the excitement of pleasure, but to be free from its vices and ill effects,—to have the sweet, and leave the bitter untasted,—that has been my study," even though "the preachers tell us that this is impossible." He has lived a life of moderation and pleasure, just as Dr. Wortle believably succeeds in his quest to maintain his self-respect (and his prosperity). Wortle learns something, too—a friend persuades him not to take this conflict as a reason to humiliate his enemies. A happy ending, as so often with Trollope, amounts to accepting ambivalence and learning a bit of wisdom.

What I like about the novel, apart from Trollope's self-portrait, is his fluent use of the materials at hand: he was visiting with his wife in Sussex—he made this his setting. It was raining almost every day; stuck inside, he wrote a novel. He knew he tended to be proud and argumentative—he made himself his protagonist. He carries it off because, at sixty-four and with plenty of experience, he is expert at novel-writing—in laying out the story, in analyzing Wortle, in parsing moral complexities, in deploying his minor characters so that they stand out but do not take over.

Fluency is a notable quality in older writers. One of my favorite examples is *The Fountain Overflows*, Rebecca West's semiautobiographical depiction of a pianist mother, a troubled politician father, and their three musical daughters. The narrative moves smoothly through a number of years, taking in the rivalries among the daughters, the mother's efforts to cope, and the father's mysterious breakdown as he abandons his family and ruins his career. It is a stylistic marvel, but perhaps its most notable quality is wise empathy—the author, in her mid-sixties, older than the parents in the novel, enters deeply, and with apparent ease, into the minds of each of her characters. She seems to understand, retrospectively, not only what has motivated their actions in the novel but also the political and social currents of the world they live in, as well as the musical expertise of the mother and the musical educations of the daughters. The reader cannot help but feel that the fountain—of wisdom—truly is overflowing as she reads this book.

Some novelists (perhaps West among them) know that books written in late life are their masterpieces. In 2011 and 2012, two well-known and prolific American novelists, Alice Hoffman and Edmund White, published *The Dovekeepers* and *Jack Holmes and His Friend*. Hoffman's novel, which she worked on for five years, concerns the conquest of the Jews by the Romans at Masada in the 70s AD. Hoffman depicts five women whose lives intersect as the Jews gather at the fortress and then commit mass suicide. Although her style is modern, Hoffman beautifully and convincingly portrays how these women would have understood their world and themselves. It is Hoffman's most ambitious novel—maybe amazingly ambitious, given the mythic dimensions of the events she is portraying. It is a sobering subject; when I asked Hoffman what keeps her going, she replied,

I've always felt that writing is my version of the fairy tale task of spinning straw into gold, taking the sorrows and losses of the real world and fashioning them into something beautiful and meaningful. Writing is illumination. I think in the end, it's a spiritual act. Continuing to write is not about adding "more books"; it's about a life in which writing serves a purpose that can't be replaced by anything else. The other issue for me—it's not as if I have one story, or one philosophy I want to express. Writing is about asking questions, and finding out the answers, and that never really ends.

Edmund White's novel, like West's, is retrospective: the narrative follows Jack Holmes from his years at the University of Michigan to his life in New York City, where he gradually discovers that he is gay, and falls unrequitedly in love with another young man he meets, Will Wright. The point of view shifts back and forth as Jack and Will mature in their connected but separate worlds of gay life and straight life. The novel is explicit, almost clinically so, about Jack's sex life. White, who was seventy-two when the novel was published, successful, and accepted, uses the freedom he has earned to investigate varieties of human experience that were once taboo. Perhaps it is for this reason that White says, "I feel that I've never yet written a novel I thought was good enough. It's like painting—it takes a lifetime to master. Titian, Rembrandt just got better and in our times Hockney and Lucian Freud. *Jack Holmes and His Friend* was my first novel that seemed like a 'real novel.'"

Nevertheless, we older novelists, however we feel about the progress of our wisdom and skills, are often haunted by earlier work. My favorite example of this is Upton Sinclair, who is now best known for the muck-raking novels he wrote in the early twentieth century, even though at sixty he began to publish what he considered his greatest literary accomplishment, the Lanny Budd series—eleven novels that open in 1913, just before World War I, and follow Lanny through the halls of wealth and power for the next forty years. The first volume is 746 pages long, readable and utterly convincing. Sinclair writes with equal eloquence and expertise about Lanny's arms-dealing father, his fashionable mother, the progress of the world war, and dozens of other topics, as they arise and are observed and experienced by a teenage boy. Volume 3, *Dragon's Teeth*, won the 1942 Pulitzer Prize. But the Lanny Budd series has sunk without a trace. Although the novels were successful in their day, Sinclair is still located in our minds in 1906—his style, sharp but amused and leisurely, was routed by the more aggressive and idiosyncratic voices of Roth, Mailer, or Vidal.

David Lodge, who has written thirty-seven books of fiction and literary criticism, once offered me his thoughts on the anxieties of older authors:

I'm inclined to think that seventy is the watershed now, beyond which a writer's ability to go on writing and publishing becomes noteworthy. There may be an economic motive, of course, but it is rarely just economic: to continue to earn money by your pen contributes to your self-esteem even if you don't really need it anymore. But if you are a literary writer, there is a deeper psychological need to go on writing and publishing. Publishing is vital of course: to go on writing books that nobody wants to publish is a fate we all fear. So is being rubbished or ignored when one's work is published. Stopping voluntarily would be a safer and more dignified option—and yet few aging writers take it. Why? Because we become addicted to writing and publishing books, though the process gets harder and harder, more and more anxiety provoking, less and less truly enjoyable—or so it seems to me. Penelope Fitzgerald—a notable veteran novelist—once said in my hearing, "I don't enjoy writing novels, but I enjoy having written one."

All of us in our sixties and seventies might say, "If I am so wise, why don't they care?"

Upon the publication of her thirty-eighth novel, *Mudwoman*, Joyce Carol Oates told the *Guardian*, "Not writing? No, the thing is, we all love storytelling, and as a writer you get to tell stories all the time." Irish novel-ist Maeve Binchy (thirty-eight novels and collections of stories) seemed to agree. She once wrote, "I will never run out of ideas: if you look at people's faces in airports, cafes, on trains, in the street you can see stories written there. Is that man afraid his wife is unfaithful? Does that woman wish she had the courage to start dating again? It's written everywhere if you look."

I, too, find ideas proliferating. I used to say that I had had fourteen ideas and written thirteen books—one book contained two novellas, and therefore two ideas. Now the books are way behind the ideas—a horse escaping Auteuil and settling in Paris? Why not? Three YA novels about a young man's Vietnam War experi-ence? Great idea! Five siblings grow up on an Iowa farm during the Depression. Why just a novel—why not a trilogy? If Trollope could write a novel in five weeks, can I do it too? But the ideas are not the pleasure; the pleasure is smaller and more specific—it is exactly that feeling when I am working at my desk that a word or an idea is coming alive. I remember when I was pondering the state of mind of Abby Lovitt, the fourteen-year-old protagonist of my YA horse series. It is New Year's Eve. She has become impatient with her parents and envi-ous of the adventures her friends are having, but also fearful—she is at that point in adolescence where you feel the world opening around you, willy-nilly, and you wonder whether you have the courage to embrace it. How would she like to be spending the evening? The first thing I imagined was a girl on a horse in a moonlit field, dangerous in California, so I listed the dangers. But this is a dream, not a reality. I wrote,

> The only thing I could think of was something I couldn't do, that no one did—it was riding my horse across a field lit by the full moon, no danger anywhere, no holes or cliffs or wild animals, just a long, smooth gallop, me leaning forward in my two-point position, hearing his breathing, feeling his warmth, sensing his strides as they opened and closed, my hands light on the reins, his mouth light in my hands. The old year would disappear into the new one easy as you please, marked only by a jump in a fence line, up and over and onward.

What I didn't know before I developed my image was that she wanted to observe the new year, but not to make a big deal of it, that in this as in everything else, what is important to Abby is knowing her own mind. Whether this image has any power for anyone else, I have no idea, but I sat back and felt a rush of pleasure—words and feelings had coalesced, an image I had never thought of before was new on the page, talking back to me. Stories intrigue me, as they do Joyce Carol Oates and Maeve Binchy, but what keeps me going is something almost mechanical—the sense of previously disparate parts locking together, becoming one, and giving off energy.

I think this is what Russell Banks was getting at when he observed, "I guess as long as there remain mysteries that I can penetrate only by means of writing, I'll keep writing. The process takes me deeper into what it is to be human than any other way of thinking can. . . . The discipline, tradition, and all the requirements of the art make me smarter, more imaginative, and more honest than I am at any other time in my life. As long as that's the case, I'll keep at it." Indeed, how could such a mental tool be voluntarily abandoned?

But there is another factor, too, which is that Abby Lovitt and her family were my friends as well as my creations. I gossiped about them to others, I wondered about their motivations, I wished them well (most of the time—Dad sometimes drove me crazy, and I had sympathy with Abby's impatience at her mother's resolute indifference to fashion). Even as I was generating them, they seemed already to exist, already to have aspirations and opinions and dilemmas that I was exploring, not creating. This is a common feeling among novelists—Dickens, for example, sometimes wept when he parted company with his characters. Francine Prose, when she published *My New American Life*, a very funny novel about a young Albanian woman who comes to the US during the Bush-Cheney years and can't help noticing how the US and Albania compare and contrast, said, "One reason to write fiction is that you can have imaginary friends, the way you did as a small child and were expected to grow out of. You can even make new imaginary friends, and it won't mean that you are crazy, but that you are writer! I find that as I get older, I still value and enjoy the company of my imaginary friends, even or especially the awful ones." Yes, especially the awful ones, the Mr. Gradgrinds, the Uriah Heeps. It is so alluring to see the world through their eyes, to acknowledge the uncomfortable kinship we feel to their greed or their malevolence. They keep us company, if by company we mean that they are always doing something significant or stimulating or meaningful. Unlike our human friends, unlike ourselves, they never devolve into the routine.

Anthony Trollope's oddest novel was surely *The Fixed Period*, written not long before he died and published afterward. It was his only foray into science fiction (it takes place in 1980), and the only book he wrote in the first person. Trollope makes his customary use of an (almost) insoluble moral dilemma—a utopian society has been founded not far from New Zealand; the land is fertile, the people are prosperous, and they have a peculiar demographic—the founders are all healthy men and women in their twenties and thirties. With the self-confidence of the young, they decide to institute a revolutionary system in which people past the age of productivity will not get pensions or live off their children, but will be escorted to a luxurious "college," where they will reside for a year before undergoing "a change probably for the better . . . an alteration of our circumstances, by which our condition may be immeasurably improved." The change will take place through judicious application of bloodletting and morphine, and *The Fixed Period*'s prime minister and narrator, Neverbend, is convinced that with plenty of preparation and the right sort of indoctrination, the inhabitants of the island can be brought to embrace the new system. The problem is that Neverbend's best friend, Crassweller, must be the first to go. As the time approaches, Crassweller, nine years older than Neverbend, and in perfect prosperous health, isn't sure that he wants to act on principle. Trollope's comic awareness of the absurdities of his subject is one of the pleasures of the novel. He also understands the practical dilemmas that the youthful instigators of the system had not foreseen—Crassweller has a marriageable daughter. How is she to view the demise of her father, and what do possible suitors think about her inheritance? Neverbend, the optimist, specializes in a sort of Orwellian Newspeak. He cringes every time someone refers to Crassweller's fate as "murder" or even euthanasia. Trollope does again what he does so well—he balances the narrative on the edge, giving arguments to both sides that are logical and full of feeling. If he did indeed tell his son, as Victoria Glendinning reports in her biography, that he meant every word of it, then I think he was wrestling with these issues of "why go on" until he could, in fact, go on no longer, and doing so in a way that belied the very premise of his novel—at sixty-seven, he may have agreed with Neverbend, but he is a Crassweller type—enterprising and experimental, readily imagining a different world, and willing to tackle a difficult subject.

Say It Ain't So, Huck

So I broke my leg. Doesn't matter how—since the accident I've heard plenty of broken-leg tales, and, I'm telling you, I didn't realize that walking down the stairs, walking down hills, dancing in high heels, or stamping your foot on the brake pedal could be so dangerous. At any rate, like numerous broken-legged intellectuals before me, I found the prospect of three months in bed in the dining room rather seductive from a book-reading point of view, and I eagerly got started. Great novels piled up on my table, and right at the top was *The Adventures of Huckleberry Finn*, which, I'm embarrassed to admit, I hadn't read since junior high school. The novel took me a couple of days (it was longer than I had remembered), and I closed the cover stunned. Yes, stunned. Not, by any means, by the artistry of the book but by the notion that this is the novel all American literature grows out of, that this is a great novel, that this is even a serious novel.

Although Huck had his fans at publication, his real elevation into the pantheon was worked out early in the Propaganda Era, between 1948 and 1955, by Lionel Trilling, Leslie Fiedler, T. S. Eliot, Joseph Wood Krutch, and some lesser lights, in the introductions to American and British editions of the novel and in such journals as *Partisan Review* and the *New York Times Book Review*. The requirements of Huck's installation rapidly revealed themselves: the failure of the last twelve chapters (in which Huck finds Jim imprisoned on the Phelps plantation, and Tom Sawyer is reintroduced and elaborates a cruel and unnecessary scheme for Jim's liberation) had to be diminished, accounted for, or forgiven; after that, the novel's special qualities had to be placed in the context first of other American novels (to their detriment) and then of world literature. The best bets here seemed to be Twain's style and the river setting, and the critics invested accordingly: Eliot, who had never read the novel as a boy, traded on his own childhood beside the big river, elevating Huck to the Boy, and the Mississippi to the River God, therein finding the sort of mythic resonance that he admired. Trilling liked the river god idea, too, though he didn't bother to capitalize it. He also thought that Twain, through Huck's lying, told truths, one of them being (I kid you not) that "something . . . had gone out of American life after the [Civil War], some simplicity, some innocence, some peace." What Twain himself was proudest of in the novel—his style—Trilling was glad to dub "not less than definitive in American literature. The prose of *Huckleberry Finn* established for written prose the virtues of American colloquial speech. . . . He is the master of the style that escapes the fixity of the printed page, that sounds in our ears with the immediacy of the heard voice, the very voice of unpretentious truth." The last requirement was some quality that would link Huck to other, though "lesser," American novels such as Herman Melville's *Moby-Dick*, that would possess some profound insight into the American character. Leslie Fiedler obligingly provided it when he read homoerotic attraction into the relationship between Huck and Jim, pointing out the similarity of this to such other white man–dark man friendships as those between Ishmael and Queequeg in Moby-Dick and Natty Bumppo and Chingachgook in James Fenimore Cooper's *Last of the Mohicans*.

The canonization proceeded apace: great novel (Trilling, 1950), greatest novel (Eliot, 1950), world-class novel (Lauriat Lane Jr., 1955). Sensible naysayers, such as Leo Marx, were lost in the shuffle of propaganda. But, in fact, *The Adventures of Huckleberry Finn* has little to offer in the way of greatness. There is more to be learned about the American character *from* its canonization than *through* its canonization.

•

Let me hasten to point out that, like most others, I don't hold any grudges against Huck himself. He's just a boy trying to survive. The villain here is Mark Twain, who knew how to give Huck a voice, but didn't know how to give him a novel. Twain was clearly aware of the story's difficulties. Not finished with having revisited his boyhood in *Tom Sawyer*, Twain conceived of a sequel and began composition while still working on *Tom Sawyer*'s page proofs. Four hundred pages into it, having just passed Cairo and exhausted most of his memories of Hannibal and the upper Mississippi, Twain put the manuscript aside for three years. He was facing a problem every novelist is familiar with: his original conception was beginning to conflict with the implications of the actual story. It is at this point in the story that Huck and Jim realize two things: they have become close friends, and they have missed the Ohio River and drifted into what for Jim must be the most frightening territory of all down the river, the very place Miss Watson was going to sell him to begin with. Jim's putative savior, Huck, has led him as far astray as a slave can go, and the farther they go, the worse it is going to be for him. Because the Ohio was not Twain's territory, the fulfillment of Jim's wish would necessarily lead the novel away from the artistic integrity that Twain certainly sensed his first four hundred pages possessed. He found himself writing not a boy's novel, like *Tom Sawyer*, but a man's novel, about real moral dilemmas and growth. The patina of nostalgia for a time and place, Missouri in the 1840s (not unlike former president Ronald Reagan's nostalgia for his own boyhood, when "Americans got along"), had been transformed into actual longing for a timeless place of friendship and freedom, safe and hidden, on the big river. But the raft had floated Huck and Jim, and their author with them, into the truly dark heart of the American soul and of American history: slave country.

Twain came back to the novel and worked on it twice again, once to rewrite the chapters containing the feud between the Grangerfords and the Shepherdsons, and later to introduce the Duke and the Dauphin. It is with the feud that the novel begins to fail, because from here on the episodes are mere distractions from the true subject of the work: Huck's affection for and responsibility to Jim. The signs of this failure are everywhere, as Jim is pushed to the side of the narrative, hiding on the raft and confined to it, while Huck follows the Duke and the Dauphin onshore to the scenes of much simpler and much less philosophically taxing moral dilemmas, such as fraud. Twain was by nature an improviser, and he was pleased enough with these improvisations to continue. When the Duke and the Dauphin finally betray Jim by selling him for forty dollars, Huck is shocked, but the fact is, neither he nor Twain has come up with a plan that would have saved Jim in the end. Tom Sawyer does that.

Considerable critical ink has flowed over the years in an attempt to integrate the Tom Sawyer chapters with the rest of the book, but it has flowed in vain. As Leo Marx points out, and as most readers sense intuitively, once Tom reappears, "Most of those traits which made [Huck] so appealing a hero now disappear. It should be added at once that Jim doesn't mind too much. The fact is that he has undergone a similar transformation. On the raft he was an individual, man enough to denounce Huck when Huck made him the victim of a practical joke. In the closing episode, however, we lose sight of Jim in the maze of farcical invention." And the last twelve chapters are boring, a sure sign that an author has lost the battle between plot and theme and is just filling in the blanks.

As with all bad endings, the problem really lies at the beginning, and at the beginning of *The Adventures of Huckleberry Finn* neither Huck nor Twain takes Jim's desire for freedom at all seriously; that is, they do not accord it the respect that a man's passion deserves. The sign of this is that not only do the two never cross the Mississippi to Illinois, a free state, but they hardly even consider it. In both *Tom Sawyer* and *Huckleberry Finn*, the Jackson's Island scenes show that such a crossing, even in secret, is both possible and routine, and even though it would present legal difficulties for an escaped slave, these would certainly pose no more hardship than locating the mouth of the Ohio and then finding passage up it. It is true that there could have been slave catchers in pursuit (though the novel ostensibly takes place in the 1840s and the Fugitive Slave Act was not passed until 1850), but Twain's moral failure, once Huck and Jim link up, is never even to account for their choice to go down the river rather than across it. What this reveals is that for all his lip service to real attachment between white boy and Black man, Twain really saw Jim as no more than Huck's sidekick, homoerotic or otherwise. All the claims that are routinely made for the book's humanitarian power are, in the end, simply absurd. Jim is never autonomous, never has a vote, always finds his purposes subordinate to Huck's, and, like every good sidekick, he never minds. He grows ever more passive and also more affectionate as Huck and the Duke and the Dauphin and Tom (and Twain) make ever more use of him for their own purposes. But this use they make of him is not supplementary; it is integral to Twain's whole conception of the novel. Twain thinks that Huck's affection is a good enough reward for Jim.

The sort of meretricious critical reasoning that has raised Huck's paltry good intentions to a "strategy of subversion" (David L. Smith) and a "convincing indictment of slavery" (Eliot) precisely mirrors the same sort of meretricious reasoning that white people use to convince themselves that they are not "racist." If Huck *feels* positive toward Jim, and *loves* him, and thinks of him as a man, then that's enough. He doesn't actually have to act in accordance with his feelings. White Americans always think racism is a feeling, and they reject it or they embrace it. To most Americans, it seems more honorable and nicer to reject it, so they do, but they almost invariably fail to understand that how they feel means very little to Black Americans, who understand racism as a way of structuring American culture, American politics, and the American economy. To invest *The Adventures of Huckleberry Finn* with "greatness" is to underwrite a very simplistic and evasive theory of what racism is and to promulgate it, philosophically, in

157

schools and the media as well as in academic journals. Surely the discomfort of many readers, Black and white, and the censorship battles that have dogged *Huck Finn* in the last twenty years are understandable in this context. No matter how often the critics "place in context" Huck's use of the word *nigger*, they can never excuse or fully hide the deeper racism of the novel—the way Twain and Huck use Jim because they really don't care enough about his desire for freedom to let that desire change their plans. And to give credit to Huck suggests that the only racial insight Americans of the nineteenth or twentieth century are capable of is a recognition of the obvious—that Blacks, slave and free, are human.

•

Ernest Hemingway, thinking of himself, as always, once said that all American literature grew out of *Huck Finn*. It undoubtedly would have been better for American literature, and American culture, if our literature had grown out of one of the best-selling novels of all time, another American work of the nineteenth century, *Uncle Tom's Cabin*, which for its portrayal of an array of thoughtful, autonomous, and passionate Black characters leaves Huck Finn far behind. *Uncle Tom's Cabin* was published in 1852, when Twain was seventeen, still living in Hannibal and contributing to his brother's newspapers, still sympathizing with the South, nine years before his abortive career in the

Confederate Army. *Uncle Tom's Cabin* was the most popular novel of its era, universally controversial. In 1863, when Harriet Beecher Stowe visited the White House, Abraham Lincoln condescended to remark to her, "So this is the little lady who made this great war."

The story, familiar to most nineteenth-century Americans, either through the novel or through the many stage adaptations that sentimentalized Stowe's work, may be sketched briefly: A Kentucky slave, Tom, is sold to pay off a debt to a slave trader, who takes him to New Orleans. On the boat trip downriver, Tom is purchased by the wealthy Augustine St. Clare at the behest of his daughter, Eva. After Eva's death, and then St. Clare's, Tom is sold again, this time to Simon Legree, whose remote plantation is the site of every form of cruelty and degradation. The novel was immediately read and acclaimed by any number of excellent judges: Charles Dickens, George Eliot, Leo Tolstoy, George Sand—the whole roster of nineteenth-century liberals whose work we read today and try to persuade ourselves that *Huck Finn* is equal to. English novelist and critic Charles Kingsley thought *Uncle Tom's Cabin* the best novel ever written. These writers honored Stowe's book for all its myriad virtues. One of these was her adept characterization of a whole world of whites and Blacks who find themselves gripped by slavery, many of whose names have entered the American language as expressions—not only Uncle Tom himself but Simon Legree and, to a lesser extent, little Eva and the Black child Topsy. The characters appear, one after another, vivified by their attitudes, desires, and opinions as much as by their histories and their fates. Surely Augustine St. Clare, Tom's owner in New Orleans, is an exquisite portrayal of a humane but indecisive man, who knows what he is doing but not how to stop it. Surely Cassy, a fellow slave whom Tom meets on the Legree plantation, is one of the great angry women in all of literature—not only bitter, murderous, and nihilistic but also intelligent and enterprising. Surely the midlife spiritual journey of Ophelia St. Clare, Augustine's Yankee cousin, from self-confident ignorance to affectionate understanding is most convincing, as is Topsy's parallel journey from ignorance and self-hatred to humanity. The ineffectual Mr. Shelby and his submissive, and subversive, wife; the slave trader Haley; Tom's wife, Chloe; Augustine's wife, Marie; Legree's overseers, Samba and Quimbo—good or evil, they all live.

As for Tom himself, we all know what an "Uncle Tom" is, except we don't. The popular Uncle Tom sucks up to the master and exhibits bovine patience. The real Uncle Tom is both a realist and a man of deep principle. When he is sold by Mr. Shelby in Kentucky, he knows enough of Shelby's affairs to know that what his master asserts is true: it's Tom who must go, or the whole estate will be sold off for debt, including Tom's wife and three children. Later, on the Legree estate, his religious faith tells him that the greatest danger he finds there is not to his life but to his soul. His logic is impeccable. He holds fast to his soul, in the face of suffering, in a way that even nonbelievers like myself must respect. In fact, Tom's story eerily prefigures stories of spiritual solace through deep religious belief that have come out of both the Soviet Gulag and the Nazi concentration camp in the same way that the structure of power on Legree's plantation, and the suffering endured there, forecasts and duplicates many stories of recent genocides.

The power of *Uncle Tom's Cabin* is the power of brilliant analysis married to great wisdom of feeling. Stowe never forgets the logical end of any relationship in which one person is the subject and the other is the object. No matter how the two people feel, or what their intentions are, the logic of the relationship is inherently tragic and traps both parties until the false subject/object relationship is ended. Stowe's most oft-repeated and potent representation of this inexorable logic is the forcible separation of family members, especially of mothers from children. Eliza, faced with the sale of her child, Harry, escapes across the breaking ice of the Ohio River. Lucy, whose ten-month-old is sold behind her back, kills herself. Prue, who has been used for breeding, must listen to her last child cry itself to death because her mistress won't let her save it; she falls into alcoholism and thievery and is finally whipped to death. Cassy, prefiguring a choice made by one of the characters in Toni Morrison's *Beloved*, kills her last child so that it won't grow up in slavery. All of these women have been promised something by their owners—love, education, the privilege and joy of raising their children—but, owing to slavery, all of these promises have been broken. The grief and despair these women display is no doubt what T. S. Eliot was thinking of when he superciliously labeled *Uncle Tom's Cabin* "sensationalist propaganda," but, in fact, few critics in the nineteenth century ever accused Stowe of making up or even exaggerating such stories. One group of former slaves who were asked to comment on Stowe's depiction of slave life said that she had failed to portray the very worst, and Stowe herself was afraid that if she told some of what she had heard from escaped slaves and other informants during her eighteen years in Cincinnati, the book would be too dark to find any readership at all.

Stowe's analysis does not stop with the slave owners and traders, or with the slaves themselves. She understands perfectly that slavery is an economic system embedded in America as a whole, and she comments ironically on Christian bankers in New York whose financial dealings result in the sale of slaves, on Northern politicians who promote the capture of escaped slaves for the sake of the public good, on ministers of churches who give the system a Christian stamp of approval. One of Stowe's most skillful techniques is her method of weaving a discussion of slavery into the dialogue of her characters. Especially interesting is a conversation Mark Twain could have paid attention to. Augustine St. Clare and his abolitionist cousin, Ophelia, are discussing his failure to act in accordance with his feelings of revulsion against slavery. After entertaining Ophelia's criticisms for a period, Augustine points out that Ophelia herself is personally disgusted by Black people and doesn't like to come into contact with them. He says, "You would think no harm in a child's caressing a large dog, even if he was black . . . custom with us does what Christianity ought to do,—obliterates the feeling of personal prejudice." When Ophelia takes over the education of Topsy, a child who has suffered a most brutal previous upbringing, she discovers that she can do nothing with her until she takes her, literally, to her bosom. But personal relationships do not mitigate the evils of slavery; Ophelia makes sure to give Topsy her freedom.

Stowe also understands that the real root of slavery is that it is profitable as well as customary. Augustine and his brother live with slavery because it is the system they know and because they haven't the imagination to live without it. Simon Legree embraces slavery because he can make money from it and because it gives him even more absolute power over his workers than he could find in the North or in England.

•

The very heart of nineteenth-century American experience and literature, the nature and meaning of slavery, is finally what Twain cannot face in *The Adventures of Huckleberry Finn*. As Jim and Huck drift down Twain's beloved river, the author finds himself nearing what must have been a crucial personal nexus: how to reconcile the felt memory of boyhood with the cruel implications of the social system within which that boyhood was lived. He had avoided this problem for the most part in *Tom Sawyer*: slaves hardly impinge on the lives of Tom and the other boys. But once Twain allows Jim a voice, this voice must speak in counterpoint to Huck's voice and must raise issues that cannot easily be resolved, either personally or culturally. Harriet Beecher Stowe, New Englander, daughter of Puritans and thinkers, active in the abolitionist movement and in the effort to aid and educate escaped slaves, had no such personal conflict when she sat down to write *Uncle Tom's Cabin*. Nothing about slavery was attractive to her either as a New Englander or as a resident of Cincinnati for almost twenty years. Her lack of conflict is apparent in the clarity of both the style and substance of the novel.

Why, then, we may ask, did *Uncle Tom's Cabin*, for all its power and popularity, fail to spawn American literature? Fail, even, to work as a model for how to draw passionate, autonomous, and interesting Black literary characters? Fail to keep the focus of the American literary imagination on the central dilemma of the American experience: race? Part of the reason is certainly that the public conversation about race and slavery that had been a feature of antebellum American life fell silent after the Civil War. Perhaps the answer is to be found in *The Adventures of Huckleberry Finn*: everyone opted for the ultimate distraction, lighting out for the territory. And the reason is to be found in *Uncle Tom's Cabin*: that's where the money was.

But so what? These are only authors, after all, and once a book is published, the author can't be held accountable for its role in the culture. For that we have to blame the citizens themselves, or their teachers, or *their* teachers, the arbiters of critical taste. In "Melodramas of Beset Manhood: How Theories of American Fiction Exclude Women Authors," the scholar Nina Baym has already detailed how the canonization of a very narrow range of white, Protestant, middle-class male authors (Twain, Hawthorne, Melville, Emerson, etc.) has misrepresented our literary life—first by defining the only worthy American literary subject as "the struggle of the individual against society [in which] the essential quality of America comes to reside in its unsettled wilderness and the opportunities that such a wilderness offers to the individual as the medium on which he may inscribe, unhindered, his own destiny and his own nature," and then by casting women, and especially women writers (specialists in the "flagrantly bad best-seller," according to Leslie Fiedler), as the enemy. In such critical readings, all other themes and modes of literary expression fall out of consideration as "un-American." There goes *Uncle Tom's Cabin*, there goes Edith Wharton, there goes domestic life as a subject, there go almost all the best-selling novelists of the nineteenth century and their readers, who were mostly women. The real loss, though, is not to our literature but to our culture and ourselves, because we have lost the subject of how the various social groups who may not escape to the wilderness are to get along in society; and, in the case of *Uncle Tom's Cabin*, the hard-nosed, unsentimental dialogue about race that we should have been having since before the Civil War. Obviously, *Uncle Tom's Cabin* is no more the last word on race relations than *The Brothers Karamazov* or *David Copperfield* is on any number of characteristically Russian or English themes and social questions. Some of Stowe's ideas about inherent racial characteristics (whites: cold, heartless; Blacks: naturally religious and warm) are bad and have been exploded. One of her solutions to the American racial conflicts that she foresaw, a colony in Africa, she later repudiated. Nevertheless, her views about many issues were brilliant, and her heart was wise. She gained the respect and friendship of many men and women of goodwill, Black and white, such as Frederick Douglass, the civil-rights activist Mary Church Terrill, the writer and social activist James Weldon Johnson, and W.E.B. Du Bois. What she did was find a way to talk about slavery and family, power and law, life and death, good and evil, North and South. She truly believed that all Americans together had to find a solution to the problem of slavery in which all were implicated. When her voice, a courageously public voice—as demonstrated by the public arguments about slavery that rage throughout *Uncle Tom's Cabin*—fell silent in our culture and was replaced by the secretive voice of Huck Finn, who acknowledges Jim only when they are alone on the raft together out in the middle of the big river, racism fell out of the public world and into the private one, where whites think it really is, but Blacks know it really isn't.

•

Should *Huckleberry Finn* be taught in the schools? The critics of the Propaganda Era laid the groundwork for the universal inclusion of the book in school curriculum, by declaring it great. Although they pre-dated the current generation of politicized English professors, this was clearly a political act, because the entry of *Huck Finn* into classrooms sets the terms of the discussion of racism and American history, and sets them very low: all you have to do to be a hero is acknowledge that your poor sidekick is human; you don't actually have to act in the interests of his humanity. Arguments about censorship have been regularly turned into nonsense by appeals to Huck's "greatness." Moreover, so much critical thinking has gone into defending Huck so that he can be great, so that American literature can be found different from and maybe better than Russian or English or French literature, that the very integrity of the critical enterprise has been called into question. That most readers intuitively reject the last twelve chapters of the novel on the grounds of tedium or triviality is clear from the fact that so many critics have turned themselves inside out to defend them. Is it so mysterious that criticism has failed in our time after being so robust only a generation ago? Those who cannot be persuaded that *The Adventures of Huckleberry Finn* is a great novel have to draw *some* conclusion.

I would rather my children read *Uncle Tom's Cabin*, even though it is far more vivid in its depiction of cruelty than *Huck Finn*, and this is because Stowe's novel is clearly and unmistakably a tragedy. No whitewash, no secrets, but evil, suffering, imagination, endurance, and redemption—just like life. Like little Eva, who eagerly but fearfully listens to the stories that her family tried to keep from her, about the slaves, our children want to know what is going on, what has gone on, and what we intend to do about it. If "great" literature has any purpose, it is to help us face up to our responsibilities instead of enabling us to avoid them once again by lighting out for the territory.

Thoughts on *My Ántonia*

Willa Cather was not a flashy stylist, and though she was ambitious for her work, she did not attach it to a publicity-worthy life like some of her contemporaries, such as Ernest Hemingway or F. Scott Fitzgerald. Cather's first book of poetry came out in 1903, when she was twenty-nine, her first book of stories when she was thirty-one. Her last novel appeared in 1940, and a volume of three more stories was published in 1948, shortly after she died. Forty-five years is a long career for a novelist, but she possessed an intensity of observation and a curiosity about human psychology, especially as it relates to nature, that never waned. *My Ántonia* is one of her best-loved books, and it displays all the characteristics that make Cather both elusive and fascinating, even as it depicts a world that vanished almost as soon as the novel was published.

Willa Cather was born in an interesting spot in the mountains of Virginia, near Winchester, on the banks of a tributary of the Potomac, Back Creek. The family properties (one owned by her grandfather, another given to her father by her grandfather) were about ninety miles from Washington, DC, and fifty miles from prosperous plantation regions like Loudon County, but, perhaps especially after the Civil War, it was difficult to make a living in the mountains, and dangerous because of tuberculosis outbreaks, so Cather's father and mother, Charles and Mary Virginia, took Willa and the other children (eventually there were seven in all) to rural Nebraska. After their first winter in the country, they settled in Red Cloud, a new town six miles north of the Kansas border and about halfway between the northwestern corner of Missouri and the northeastern corner of Colorado. Willa was about to turn ten. In Nebraska, the Cathers, immigrants from Virginia, immediately encountered a huge population of other immigrants from more distant and perhaps more romantic—to Willa—places: Norway, Sweden, France, Bohemia, Mexico. A sense of the world that compelled Cather for the rest of her life began to develop, a sense of the world that is deeply American, simultaneously local and exploratory, rustic and cosmopolitan.

Cather's early prairie novels were published over the course of six years that were extremely eventful in American and world history—*O Pioneers!* in 1913, *The Song of the Lark* in 1915, and *My Ántonia* in 1918. She did not address the issues of World War I until her next novel, *One of Ours*, published in 1922. (It won the Pulitzer Prize in 1923.) But in all four works, the main characters Alexandra, Thea, Ántonia, and Claude wrestle with more or less the same question, maybe the essential question of the twentieth century—to stay or to go, and if so, how and why?

O Pioneers!, *The Song of the Lark*, and *My Ántonia* (and also the first half of *One of Ours*) are linked by place, not by character—unlike Émile Zola's or Anthony Trollope's series, Cather does not write about characters who are related to or know one another. As a result, once we have read the early novels, we feel as though we are watching the characters from a distance as they put their lives together, move across the landscape. Other prominent and best-selling authors in the first two decades of the twentieth century were looking at Europe and high society (Henry James, Edith Wharton), or the future (H. G. Wells), or the trials of the urban poor (Upton Sinclair, Winston Churchill— not *the* Winston Churchill, but a best-selling, now unknown, novelist from St. Louis). Authors who wrote about the West wrote books like Zane Grey's *The Lone Star Ranger*, disparaged by critics as unrealistic and unnecessarily violent. Cather, who began her career in magazine publishing, knew perfectly well what was popular, and what was respected, but, like Alexandra, Thea, and Ántonia, she was determined to go her own way. As a result, her novels stick in the reader's mind as flickering memories of places we may never have seen with our own eyes.

O Pioneers! and *The Song of the Lark* are told from the omniscient point of view. *O Pioneers!* begins with a long shot of a snowstorm and a young boy crying because his kitten has gotten away from him; it then homes in on Alexandra, the protagonist, who will eventually, and almost by herself, develop the family farm. *The Song of the Lark*, which focuses on Thea, a child of eleven, begins with a visit from the town doctor, who makes a house call and discovers that Thea has pneumonia. We are asked to contemplate Thea through the lens of her family, not her landscape—her family and friends are what she must leave in order to achieve renown as a musician. For *My Ántonia*, Cather chose a more conversational first-person point of view—in the introduction, Cather says that she'd once met an old acquaintance on a train across Iowa; they'd reminisced about a striking girl whom they both remembered fondly. Cather thought she would like to write about her, but Jim Burden, now a lawyer in New York, had already set down his memories of Ántonia. He sent them to Cather, and they formed the novel.

Jim is a stand-in for Cather's own voice. In Red Cloud, Cather was old enough to remember Virginia and to observe the uniqueness of her new environment, as well as the energy and hardships of the immigrants around her. She thrived in school and planned to be a doctor—she dissected frogs, kept her hair short, and even signed her name "William Cather." After giving a celebrated high school graduation speech, she went to college at the University of Nebraska in Lincoln. In her biography of Cather, Hermione Lee points out that Cather also felt a sense of constriction in Red Cloud, and that her see-saw of ambition and constriction was common to writers who were growing up in small towns at the same time she was, such as Sinclair Lewis, Sherwood Anderson, and Theodore Dreiser. Life at the end of the nineteenth century meant easy rail transportation, lots of magazines, and plenty of books, but they came with the sense that one was an outsider. They also came with the sense that an outsider could get to the inside with some effort.

At the University of Nebraska, Cather was ambitious in her studies and in her extracurricular literary activities, one of which was editing the *Hesperian*, the university literary journal. She studied with a journalism professor who was managing editor of the local town paper, and eventually he hired her to write reviews of itinerant theater productions put on by companies that passed through Red Cloud and Lincoln. (Her column was called "The Passing Show.") Her reviews were often harsh, and because the acting companies were traveling from coast to coast, she became famous, or notorious, which led to a job with a magazine based in Pittsburgh called *Home Monthly*. When she left Nebraska for Pennsylvania, she was twenty-two.

•

In the novel, Jim is ten, sent from Virginia, where both of his parents have died, to his grandparents in Black Hawk. Since he is the same age Cather was when she first experienced Nebraska, his immediate observations are telling—one is, "The only thing very noticeable about Nebraska was that it was still, all day long, Nebraska." And his whole way of perceiving the world is changed by the emptiness of the landscape: "I had the feeling that the world was left behind, that we had got over the edge of it, and were outside man's juris-diction." His grandparents are loving and kind, their cowboy hired man friendly and amusing, and almost as soon as he wanders out of the house and over to the distant garden, Jim realizes that he is "entirely happy" and has a revelation: "At any rate, that is happiness; to be dissolved into something complete and great."

His sense of being right at home is contrasted to the difficulties of his nearest neighbors, the Shimerdas, whom he had seen on the train and who have just immigrated from Bohemia (now the western half of the Czech Republic, which was, in the 1880s, under the control of the Austro-Hungarian Empire). Even on the train he had noticed Ántonia, who is twelve or thirteen, and he soon gets drawn into her life and the life of her family, which is difficult, partly because they have bought an undeveloped property sight unseen and partly because Mr. Shimerda never wanted to leave Bohemia in the first place. And so Ántonia must do something similar to Alexandra in *O Pioneers!*: make her own way, but also do her best to save her family.

Cather gains a few things from ceding the narrative to a first-person male point of view—Jim is an active boy, raised without many restrictions, who can move at will in town and out in the countryside. He is not required to adhere to the same social norms as the girls are; the daughters of prosperous families have to behave like ladies, and the daughters of working families have to devote themselves to making money. He can also express all his varied feelings toward the girls he grows up with, who are much more the focus of the narrative than he is. Cather gives Jim Burden some of her own restlessness. He does well in school, goes to Lincoln, realizes that he is not cut out to be a scholar, and ends up in law school, but even as he succeeds, he cannot get his Black Hawk experiences out of his mind: "But whenever my consciousness was quickened, all those early friends were quickened within it, and in some strange way they accompanied me through all my new experiences. They were so much alive in me that I scarcely stopped to wonder whether they were alive anywhere else, or how."

It is tempting for a reader to speculate about whether a novel, especially one written in the first person, is autobiographical, and certainly Cather's uncanny ability to evoke the landscape (and the humanscape) of a town in Nebraska similar to Red Cloud invites that question, but the plot of a novel doesn't have to be autobiographical to enable vivid perceptions and feelings; in fact, I would say, when a plot is not autobiographical, the author feels a freedom of depiction that opens up the world of memory to bits and pieces that are alive but unattached to any particular history. In *O Pioneers!* and *The Song of the Lark*, Cather is interested in how

Alexandra and Thea manage to achieve the successes they seek. *My Ántonia* is much more about who Ántonia is, what it feels like to others to recognize her charisma and to love her—yes, she undergoes many trials and is successful, and Jim admires her success, but what he is really interested in is how her beauty and toughness reflect the landscape she lives in and how he feels about that. *My Ántonia* is about permanence and ephemerality and how they coexist.

•

The first time Cather mentions *My Ántonia* is in a letter to her publisher from March 1917. She is living on Bank Street in New York City. She tells her publisher that she has set aside the book she had been working on and begun another, "about the same length as *O Pioneers!*" (Willa Cather, *The Selected Letters of Willa Cather*, ed. Andrew Jewell and Janis Stout [New York: Vintage Books, 2014], 237). She is halfway through the first draft and hopes to be finished in time for an autumn 1917 publication. In the summer she goes back to Nebraska to receive an honorary doctorate, and then back to Red Cloud, perhaps for inspiration. But she can't complete the manuscript because, like most Americans, or maybe most people in the world, she is preoccupied by World War I—she writes that she thinks that the American entry into the war is the only thing that can save Europe, and maybe Russia and maybe America itself—"If we don't do this, we will have to be Prussians in the end" (240). The other letters she writes to her publisher about *My Ántonia* are focused on illustrations and binding, not on her progress or dissatisfaction or pleasure in the actual writing of the novel. When we read the novel, what is indeed amazing is how absent the war, or any sense of external danger to the world that she is writing about, is. It may be that in composing *My Ántonia*, Cather managed to successfully remove herself from the present and even more deeply immerse herself in her past.

Unfortunately, the war impinged itself on Cather's life in June 1918, when her aunt's son, G. P. Cather, was killed in France and his death listed in one of the New York newspapers (the inspiration for *One of Ours*). She immediately wrote to her aunt, lamenting G.P.'s death, but also recalling his restlessness and honoring his desire to serve a cause that she considered essential to the survival of modern society. Around the same time, she was sent the copyedited manuscript of *My Ántonia*. As with the illustrations, she is particular about the details of the style, the paper, and the layout. But she also writes to her brother, "It's a queer sort of book. It's at least not like either of the others" (258). This is maybe the best review an author can give her own work, because it indicates that the book has surprised even her, challenged her own expectations and recollections, and taught her something new.

Cather sent the proofs back to the publisher in

early August, and the book was published in October. The reviews were raves; in a letter to her brother Roscoe, Cather, always opinionated, says that she's pleased that her brother and her parents "liked this book," and she appreciates the excellent reviews, but she prefers *The Song of the Lark*, because it contains "more warmth and struggle." One reviewer, from the *Nation*, praised its "atmosphere of pure beauty." Cather scoffs: "Nonsense, its [*sic*] the atmosphere of my grandmother's kitchen, and nothing else" (261).* A hundred years later, what I take from her remarks is that one of the things critics loved about *My Ántonia* was that it recalled a world of relative human innocence and natural beauty that readers knew was disappearing, even as the book was being published, because of technology, war, urban expansion. *My Ántonia* is set, perhaps unknowingly, at a particular turning point in American history, where the plains and the mountains, people and towns, writers and readers, were simultaneously isolated and connected, able to feel the power of the landscape and also to escape it.

Jim Burden's last visit to Ántonia is a visit to her victory—she has prospered on the farm she owns with her husband; she is mother to many active and good-natured children who have inherited her health and her wildness. She is happy. A hundred years later,

---

* The line Cather quoted has not been found in the *Nation* review, so she might have been mistaking it for something else she read.

we must set her happiness into the context of the history of the West—fifteen years after the publication of *My Ántonia*, drought and dust storms brought on by the mechanized plowing of the prairies would challenge the very idea that the land should have been populated, should have been cultivated, should have succumbed to the system of monoculture. Yes, Cather was right, *My Ántonia* is a queer book, flickering with darkness and light, a true representation of its time, both in terms of wisdom and in terms of ignorance.

We read novels for suspense and drama, and *My Ántonia* has plenty of both—the Shimerdas' efforts, and those of the other immigrants whom Jim knows, are sometimes tragic, sometimes amusing, and sometimes rewarded. And there is always the pleasure of watching Cather's characters develop—she is perceptive and detailed about their motivations, about their idiosyncrasies, and about how they affect each other. But finally, it all comes back to landscape, to humans changing and being changed by the difficulties and the beauties of the world they must contend with. It is also true, though, that we read older novels differently from new ones—we read them to understand what we have lost and what we have gained, what the author knew and what she didn't know that she knew, but that we now understand shaped the world we are living in. Because of Willa Cather's intensity of observation, *My Ántonia* remains a revelation.

Gregor: My Life as a Bug

We were all introduced to The Metamorphosis *when we were young, and for a long time, it seemed to me to be an untouchable, great, and striking work; but the more times I read it, the more I wondered what it might be like if written in the third-person interior point of view, and whether there might be a way to create a happy ending, so on a whim, I wrote this.*

After some strenuous months of adjusting to and caring for the "giant dung beetle" that has unaccountably replaced their son, Gregor, the Samsa family have gone away to the country, to get some fresh air and plan for the future. The lodgers who precipitated the crisis are gone, as is the cleaning lady who has been "looking after" Gregor for the last few weeks. Gregor himself, much desiccated and weakened, but alive, has been carried out to the dustheap to ponder his metamorphosis.

All day, though sunk deeply in the stupor of profound physical weakness, Gregor had sensed the light beyond his eyelids, woven into his dreams, as it were, in the form of an uneasy awareness that soon he would wake up, that soon, all too soon, he wouldn't be able to avoid that, but it was only at dusk that he actually did rise to consciousness, and beheld the now familiar sight of his domed belly and his numerous helpless little legs glinting in the roseate shafts of sunlight that lengthened from the west down the otherwise dreary stretch of alley that ran behind the row of apartment houses.

The cleaning lady, practical and straightforward in her way, had not been much of a diagnostician and even less of an entomologist—what could she know, without education?—but the Samsas had willingly, perhaps even eagerly, accepted her certification of Gregor's death. Gregor had, too (had he not?), so disheartened was he by his sister's revulsion. (You couldn't hide such a thing, a physical reaction like that, that much was crystal clear.) Nor could you, Gregor reflected, die by wishing to. All too often, you had to wake up and live on. Make the best of things. Focus on the little physical pleasures of moving and eating and feeling a bit of a breeze and try to get through the rest.

With practiced ease, but somewhat slowed by lingering weakness, Gregor rolled from his back to his thorax, and lifted himself on legs that trembled but held. The dust and dirt that the cleaning lady had thrown out with him shifted and slid off his shining shell. His long feet sank into the dust, but it wasn't that hard to pull himself upward, nibbling a rind of cheese and a stale bit of cake and a brown apple core as he went. Slowly—it didn't matter; by himself, with none of that sense of anxiety that his parents and sister had communicated to him for the last months, he could move as he wished. And in the dark, too. The sunset had faded, and a warm redolent breeze came to his proboscis. He got to the apex of the dustheap and remembered an advertising slogan he had seen once for a sleeping nostrum—"Knit up the ravelled sleave of care—with Levy's Sleeping Draught! You'll feel better in the morning!" And he did feel better, no two ways about that. Now when he thought of his sister's reaction, well, it was her problem. Clearly, out here in the alley, he had problems of his own.

He smelled, as much as saw, the delicious odor of some rotting meat—mutton, it was—but when he stepped toward it, he toppled alarmingly forward, and then, unable to catch his balance, fell farther forward until he found himself rolling head over tail down the other side of the dustheap. He did manage to pick up the bit of mutton as he went, but only at the cost of painfully wrenching his back plates. Then he rolled out onto the cobblestones, and that was unpleasant, too— bruising his head and sides, making him ache all over, in fact. But the mutton tasted good. The thing was just to enjoy it, enjoy it at his leisure, the way they had never let him do during his whole life. And he did—he relished it bite by bite, concentrating, forgetting the pain, focusing on the pleasure.

The cobblestones were big as well as hard. How did people walk on these cobblestones? They were like hills! What were the town's engineers thinking of, building streets like this? Surely people would complain. You had to walk between them, along the seams, if you wanted to get anywhere. Gregor shook himself, and then made his way slowly, exploring with his feelers. It was a puzzle indeed, how the town had changed this way, and then he passed a large metal cavern, dark but square-shaped and raised off the stone—clearly not a door, looking more than anything like a drainpipe, but so extraordinarily large! Gregor marveled.

And then he realized. He was not nearly so large himself as they had made him out to be. Well, that was typical of them, the way they had always magnified problems. Any little change was monstrous to them. They were fearful people. He had known that—especially his mother, and his father wasn't any better, even though he hid his fear with anger. But it was hard, living at home, not to react the way they expected you to react.

He skittered with great speed and grace between the cobblestones, stopping to drink from a puddle. Cool, refreshing. The sleep and food had perked him right up. The thing was, they weren't bad people, he could see that. They did their best, given their fears, given how housebound they were—his own fears, too, why not admit that? He had expected them to change, but he hadn't really had the guts to make them change. It had all stayed more or less the same—everything unspoken, everything dictated by habit and duty. What did it matter, really, whether he was serving them, as he had when he was working, or they were serving him? Just the same tangle of anxiety and pressure and obligation and tedium. Sure, love was somewhere in there, but you had to get away to find it.

A silver light swelled over the cobblestones, and Gregor looked up to see the moon, calm and full as a plate, pause over his alley. He hadn't seen it in months, since before his metamorphosis. It was different now, though, not flat but full of facets like a giant diamond. He lifted his back pair of legs and gave a triumphant buzz of joy. Sure, the world held dangers, but hell, so what? What was that compared to setting out? Compared to the actual, authentic, bona fide transformation that lay ahead of him now?

Gregor looked up at the building. Perhaps those were his family's windows, just lighting up there on the third floor, as they returned from wherever they had been. He hoped they felt better. He wanted only good things for them, after all. He gazed for a moment, then raised his proboscis in a single salute. He was off now, down the alley to the street, and to many streets beyond. He stretched his young body, and headed down the road between the cobblestones.

Meet Jessica Mitford

Jessica Mitford's dedicated and adventuresome life is hard to comprehend in our age of cell phones, jet travel, internet searches, and political cynicism: when she wasn't allowed to go to school as a child in the 1920s and '30s, her education was therefore patchy and incomplete—something she regretted well into adulthood; when she ran off at the age of nineteen with her first husband, Esmond Romilly, to join the leftist cause in the Spanish Civil War, she really did disappear; when her first child died of measles, it was because Jessica herself had not been vaccinated; when she embraced worldwide Communism, it was because the Soviets had managed to keep huge areas of the world secret and off-limits to western eyes. In some ways, Mitford was a typical citizen of a time and place where distance was hard to traverse and knowledge of faraway locales was limited at best.

But all the Mitfords, including Jessica, are mostly famous for being uniquely at the center of their world, indeed, for the invasion of that world into the very core of their family life. And they continue to fascinate and perplex us. Jessica was the second-youngest of seven—six sisters and one brother. The eldest, Nancy, born in 1904, was a fashionable "bright young thing" in the

1920s, best friends with Evelyn Waugh until she died, and one of the great comic novelists of the twentieth century. Diana, younger than Nancy by six years, first married into the Guinness family, then, in a great scandal, left Brian Guinness for Oswald Mosley, the head of the British Union of Fascists, a vociferous supporter of Hitler throughout the 1930s. Through Diana, Jessica's favorite sister, Unity, conceived a stalker-like passion for Adolf Hitler that he used as an entrée to acceptance by English aristocracy. Although Unity shot herself when England went to war against Germany, and Diana and Oswald Mosley went to jail, Unity, Diana, and Jessica's mother remained dedicated Nazis until they died. In the meantime, another sister, Deborah, married the Duke of Devonshire and became mistress of one of the largest estates in all of England. One sister, Pamela, avoided the spotlight, and the only brother, Thomas, was killed in Burma in World War II.

Jessica Mitford did not begin to write professionally until she was almost forty, but when she did, she had plenty to write about. Her first book, *Hons and Rebels* (in the US, *Daughters and Rebels*) was a memoir of her childhood, her years with Esmond Romilly, and her emigration to the US. It was notable, of course, for the eccentric tale she had to tell, but became beloved for her lively style—her autobiographical voice is amused, observant, honest, and enthusiastic. She tells her tale as if it could not have gone differently, and the reader believes her.

Mitford's second book, *The American Way of Death*, was a more straightforward piece of muckraking journalism, as Mitford herself liked to call it, and it was written jointly with her husband, labor lawyer Robert Treuhaft. *The American Way of Death* was a sensation not because of its tone (though throughout her career, Mitford remained amused at the foolishness as well as the greed of great American scammers) but because of its revelations of unethical practices in the funeral industry. After *The American Way of Death*, Mitford began muckraking in earnest, and *Poison Penmanship* is a collection of articles written for various publications between 1961 and 1979. Some are lighter or more occasional than others, but all give the reader the sense that Jessica Mitford is entirely to be trusted—not only because she sees the world as it is but because she sees herself with the same skepticism.

This is not how we expect Communists to be, but from her mid-teens, Mitford dedicated herself to the work of the Left. She originally moved to San Francisco to work for the war-related Office of Price Administration, but, as she writes in her later memoir, *A Fine Old Conflict*, once there, she set out to find and join the Communist Party. Soon Treuhaft came to San Francisco, they were married, and then worked for the party, for labor causes, and for civil rights causes for the next sixteen years, until party divisions over the Soviet invasion of Hungary in 1956 drove most of the younger and more progressive members out. In the course of her time in the party, Mitford was called before the House Un-American Activities Committee and investigated by the FBI. But she expressed no regrets, and after leaving the Communist Party never hid her opinions.

If there is a more forthright, good-natured, and witty American investigative journalist, I don't know who it would be. In the course of a career that spanned almost forty years, she wrote eleven books (including a volume of letters collected after her death). Carl Bernstein, in an afterword to *Poison Penmanship*, calls her "an amateur," but she was hardly inexperienced at either reading or writing, as her many hilarious and insightful letters show. In fact, she was self-educated, as the great majority of women writers once were (including Jane Austen and Virginia Woolf)—haphazardly but effectively.

Poison Penmanship is conceived not only as a collection of occasional pieces but, since Mitford enjoyed the teaching posts she held once she was established, also as a consideration of muckraking as a form of journalism. The lengthy introduction describes how she got started writing, and gives tips—how to gather background information, how to interview (meaning how to get antagonistic interviewees to betray themselves), how to find information not available to the general public, how to recognize a blind alley, and how to organize and write the article. She also discusses potential consequences. In the section labeled "Libel," she writes, "I have often been asked whether

I have been sued for libel in the course of my writing career. The answer is no, alas." Mitford was careful to check her facts.

Mitford unabashedly wrote for money, and part of her charm in this volume is in the afterword to each piece, in which she describes how she came to the subject and what the challenges were—the challenges of writing about a silly upscale spa seem to have been greater than the challenges of writing about a surge in the rate of syphilis infection among teenagers of the 1960s and the refusal of the National Broadcasting Company to air two fairly anodyne but explicit episodes of popular programs on the subject, even though the government begged the network to do so. ("Not in the best interests of the viewing public," said NBC.) Mitford's specific argument evolves into a condemnation of the bland commerciality of network TV. One wonders what she would have made of *The Kardashians*. Above all things, Mitford liked a worthy opponent, and her weapons of choice were factual accuracy and a tone of amazement. Perhaps the best piece in here is "Let Us Now Praise Famous Writers," in which she reveals the anatomy of the scam that was "The Famous Writer's School," which was sold through magazines and coercive follow-up by "representatives," and promised personal attention to a student's manuscripts by such literary luminaries as Bennett Cerf. In this piece, Miss Mitford is a bit less amused, and the result was suitable embarrassment all around.

Mitford is straightforward in raising the question of whether muckraking journalism is effective or not at changing the world for the better. She mentions Lincoln Steffens (who eventually decided that it wasn't) and Ralph Nader (who is still at it), as well as Robert Scheer (then young), who is also still at it. She is honest about the immediate results of her own exposés—some worked better than others. From our vantage point in a time when muck is being raked (and flung) vehemently and constantly twenty-four hours a day, the question of effectiveness is overwhelmed by the question of whether any person in America with access to the media remains shockable or persuadable. In this regard, Mitford was a toiler in the muck who cared about facts and believed in the idea that her fellow citizens were generally honest and expected the same of business and government. She might have been daunted by the way that lies and spin have taken over our public discourse. But given her habit, in *Poison Penmanship*, of being thrilled by a good fight, I doubt it.

The Other Nancy Mitford

Let's pretend that we know no more of Nancy Mitford than we do of Shakespeare, that we have a tempting outline of her life with one or two intriguing details, but no family notoriety, no volumes of letters, no newspaper articles or gossip. In fact, let's pretend that Nancy Mitford's novels weren't written by the famous Nancy Mitford but by some entirely obscure Mary Smith, who happened to be a middle-class daughter of a greengrocer, possessed of ambition, eloquence, and extraordinary powers of observation. If we did so, how would the novels hold up?

There are eight of them, written over the course of thirty years. Vintage has reissued all eight: *Highland Fling* (1931), *Christmas Pudding* (1932), *Wigs on the Green* (1935), *Pigeon Pie* (1940), *The Pursuit of Love* (1945), *Love in a Cold Climate* (1949), *The Blessing* (1951), and *Don't Tell Alfred* (1960). The jokes are funny, and they are daring, tossed into the narrative in an offhand way. Sophia, the protagonist of *Pigeon Pie*, doesn't hear about the start of World War II because she has been visiting her father in Scotland, "a widowed peer, who could write his name, Maida Vale, but little else." When Sophia's wealthy husband gets involved with "the Boston Brotherhood, one of those new religions which are wafted to us every six months or so across the Atlantic," she must put up with Florence Turnbull, who remarks, "Personally, the only people I care to be very intimate with are the ones you feel would make a good third if God asked you out to dinner."

In *Wigs on the Green*, a bored married woman known as "the local beauty" is persuaded by a charming scoundrel that her potential lover is a dashing representative of eastern European royalty, when in fact he is a London office worker who has just received a small legacy. In the meantime, her husband goes to a cattle sale to buy a cow: "He bought the wrong one at an exorbitant price only to discover that his purchase was lacking in that desirable piece of anatomy—the udder." All of Mitford's characters accept infidelity as routine and unimportant, all of them are suspicious of Americans and their earnest professions of belief, and all are observant and irreverent—chaos is not only inevitable but desirable, or at least amusing.

But there is no real sense, in the prewar works, of the grandeur and sophistication Mitford would achieve in the last four. There is, in fact, considerable evidence, especially in *Wigs on the Green* and *Pigeon Pie*, that Mitford's worldview—compounded of knowing frivolity and evenhanded acceptance of the various political forces that are about to clash so tragically—is overwhelmed by her material. She can organize her story, more or less, and she can give her characters vivid life, but she can't acknowledge the meaning of their opinions or their actions. Her characters are imprisoned in a world where consequences are muffled by privilege and where all eccentricities are merely amusing. The clue to the narrowness of this world is Mitford's failure to introduce it systematically or to depict it with much detail. She writes from the center of that world, for an audience who knows what she is talking about, for whom more explanation would retard the pace of the jokes.

Between 1940 and 1946, Mitford found a deeper sense of conviction. She used it not to make her work less comic or more doctrinaire but to make it even more daring and worldly, and to round her characters into brilliant figures. One way that she did this was to turn to the very eccentric world of Uncle Matthew and Aunt Sadie, patriarch and matriarch of the irrepressible Radlett family. The Radletts are decidedly not fashionable and so odd as to require organized delineation. Uncle Matthew is an irascible, expressive, and even violent country squire whose only defense is his liveliness. He hates foreigners of every sort, loves blood sports, and alternately shouts at his children and ignores them. His great virtue as a literary character is that he is voluble and amusing, and around him the others coalesce, saying anything they please, no matter how ill-tempered, ignorant, snobbish, rude, or silly. The manner in which this distinct and lively small world of Englishness takes on and responds to the world events of the next fifteen years is the subject of *The Pursuit of Love, Love in a Cold Climate, The Blessing,* and *Don't Tell Alfred.*

The premise of *The Pursuit of Love* is as old as the English novel: a young girl from a good family is in search of a husband, except that what Linda Radlett discovers when she makes her marriage is not eternal happiness but stuffy boredom. She is in pursuit of love, not marriage, after all, and as a result she crosses the Channel and ends up in France, installed as the mistress of Fabrice Sauveterre. Fanny, the novel's narrator, links Linda's new world and the Radlett world; she has grown up with Linda, she is young, she marries a Cambridge academic and is happy with her domestic life. But as the daughter of "The Bolter," a woman who has made a career of amatory adventure, she has more varied opinions about traditional English marriage than any of the other characters in the book. Her contemplative voice gives their brasher ones a context. The result is that Mitford explores what love means in the modern world, and also that she perfects her technique of offhand commentary.

In her last four novels, Mitford does not hesitate to take on large issues. By setting the old theme of girl-in-search-of-love next to the onset of World War II, Mitford gets to question the equation that had prevailed in the English novel from the eighteenth century on, in which marriage and a good property settlement equal true love. Part of the truth of Linda and Fabrice's love is that it is fleeting—Fabrice is captured and killed during the war, and Linda dies in childbirth. Another part is that it is, indeed, "true": Fabrice's active career in the French Resistance testifies to his integrity and to his ability to distinguish between idle occupations and sincere devotion. He may live one way before the war and one way during the war, but, unlike Linda's husband, this is not due to ambivalence about the Nazis or their ideology, but rather because he is a worldly man and has a French aristocrat's refined sense of what is appropriate at any given moment. In this, he is a bit like Matthew Radlett, who colorfully deplores the idea Linda's first husband proposes—that if England is really in danger, best to just follow the money you've posted in international banks, and ride the whole thing out. Uncle Matthew has a plan for when the Germans attack his farm, and it involves both martyrdom and heavy German casualties. By 1946, the war has clarified Mitford's worldview. She is still flexible about customs and private morality, but her political views are set: extremism to either right or left is not only dangerous but silly. Those who loudly promote their views are the opportunists most likely to betray their avowals. In a chaotic world, those with the gift of observation are the most trustworthy.

In *Love in a Cold Climate*, my favorite, Mitford perfects her cool analysis of character and brings to life several simultaneously horrifying and amusing figures, none of whom she judges. Although perfectly well bred and married into the best property in England, Lady

Montdore is a monster of social-climbing shallowness. Her marriageable daughter, a reserved beauty, is dedicated to love, just like Linda Radlett, but the man she loves is Boy Dougdale, her mother's longtime companion and a well-known (at least among the children) child molester. She gets her way and marries her dreamboat. Lady Montdore is then redeemed by the heir to the estate, a gay cousin from Nova Scotia who is on the run from some of his own rent-boy adventures on the Continent. The final reconciliation is defined not in terms of property, family, or wealth, but by affection, comfort, and caretaking—no matter how peculiar or unorthodox those relationships happen to be.

A defining characteristic of Mitford's later writing is the clarity of her style. She is as straightforward and objective as Trollope. Her narrators tell their stories and are clear about the difference between what happens, how they view it, and how others view it. This style makes for smooth reading, and was pretty much outmoded when Mitford was writing. Her contemporaries—Evelyn Waugh, Graham Greene, and Anthony Powell—cultivated styles that were more original, and therefore subjective. The world, if it could be viewed at all, had to be viewed through a new lens, a necessary lens, that acknowledged the subjectivity of truth. Mitford approached the subjectivity of truth through dialogue, and what her characters say is more extreme, rude, and self-revealing than anything in Trollope or Austen; the English landscape is still there, but traditional proprieties are long gone, replaced by choices and dangers that are thoroughly modern.

Surely one of Random House's reasons for reissuing Mitford's works is that their themes and characters remain oddly current. In *The Blessing*, a Frenchman, Charles-Edouard de Valhubert, marries a pretty Englishwoman in haste; he is being sent back to the front, and wants to be sure of an heir. Grace Allingham is already engaged, but Charles-Edouard prevails, and their son is six years old by the time his father returns to make up his mind whether to continue the marriage or end it. (Since they are married at a registry office rather than in the church, divorce is an option.) What follows is a romance of misunderstandings and missed connections; and the character repeatedly sticking his spanner into the work of reconciliation is Sigi, the child, who readily understands that single parents are more likely to spoil him—his continued welfare demands that he keep them apart.

The subplot of *The Blessing* revolves, once again, around enthusiastic Americans—in this case Hector Dexter, who is representing the Marshall Plan in Europe and has failed, so far, to gain entrance to any of the more exclusive social sets. As Grace explains, "They go back to the middle of America and tell the people there, who hate foreigners anyway, that the French are undependable, and so nasty that it would be better to cut the Aid and concentrate on Italy, where they are undependable, too, but so nice, and especially on Germany, where they are dependable and so wonderful, and leave the nasty French to rot." Hector is a world-class conversation-hogging bore, and when he finally gets around to his diagnosis, it's this: "There is a malaise in this country, a spirit of discontent, of nausea, of defatigation, of successlessness around us, here in this very city of Paris, which I for one find profoundly discouraging." ("I wish I understood Americans," says Charles-Edouard. "They are very strange. So good, and yet so dull.") Mitford neatly subordinates the unfolding of Hector Dexter's activities to the reconciliation between Charles-Edouard and Grace, allowing the reader to survey the post-war landscape—social, personal, and political—without inflating or underestimating the interest of any part. The subject of her confection is, in more ways than one, betrayal. But she maintains her confectionary tone, and the result is bracingly clear and worldly.

Mitford's last novel, *Don't Tell Alfred*, returns to the Radletts and Fanny. Fanny's academic husband, Alfred, is suddenly posted to France, and required to deal with such practical political matters as a disputed set of Channel Islands that are sometimes entirely submerged. The children produced in earlier novels are now busy either exploring their world or making trouble (depending on your point of view). Uncle Matthew returns, also, a sort of venerable object of curiosity who goes to fashionable parties. High society has turned into pop culture, and Mitford's world is recognizably modern. Fabrice and Charlie, two of Fanny's sons from *The Pursuit of Love*, have made friends with Sigi from *The Blessing* and left Eton to take on the management of a working-class rock-and-roll singer. Another, David, has become a follower of a Zen master, and another, Basil, has disappeared, only to turn up a few pages later with The Bolter's newest husband—a boy his own age. These two have a plan to fleece English tourists on the Continent. Basil consistently refers to his partner as "Grandfather." Mitford abandons the traditional English comic love plot for a broader and less defined narrative arc. There is no solace in marriage, or any agreement on what love is. Although the war did not succeed in destroying prewar culture, the generation of children born during and just after the war is busy doing so.

The dilemma for Fanny is whether to interfere with the freedom her offspring have claimed and the destruction that portends. Her problem is personified by a tabloid gossip journalist, Amyas Mockbar, who makes a point of humiliating officials such as her husband in his paper, the *Daily Post*. Fanny can neither ignore Amyas nor combat him, but must wait for circumstances through which he comes to grief on his own, just as she must wait for her children to learn their own lessons, and for the French government and the English government to realize that the oft-submerged islands they're contending over aren't worth it. The novel is more episodic than the three previous novels, a structure that mimics the new, enlarged size of Fanny's world. In the earlier novels, the boundary between safety and chaos is distinct, but once the war is over and forgotten, there is no longer a boundary—only a frontier that Fanny must learn to negotiate. Published in 1960, before the Beatles, before the generation gap, *Don't Tell Alfred* remains eerily prescient about parenting and the speed of cultural change.

But is it enough that Mitford's novels are a delight to read, that they remain laugh-out-loud funny, and that they are beautifully constructed as well as daring in several ways? Could it be that they have a relevance to our modern lives that books by Mitford's contemporaries (Fitzgerald, Faulkner, Hemingway, Waugh, Greene, Anthony Powell), however great they are, no longer quite have? If Mitford's works weren't overwhelmed by her fame, would we respect them more?

The hallmark of modernity was the recognition of the subjective—that a novelist's (or an analysand's, or a regular person's) inner life shaped his or her sense of reality, and, in fact, was Reality. The assertive style of Mitford's contemporaries made this point: a reader's pleasure in their books was in being overwhelmed by an alien language that represented a more authentic worldview than old-fashioned realism. The idea that such representations were literature's primary function held sway for at least two generations, and still has powerful partisans, but what the reissue of Mitford's novels shows us is that an author can acknowledge the presence of many subjectivities. She can clear the stage by adopting a transparent style, and then let the characters contend. She can shamelessly address all sorts of issues as social dilemmas, and thereby ponder them. She can observe, as Mitford did, so acutely that her eye becomes a finely ground lens, not dimming our vision, but heightening it. Nancy Mitford wasn't the first English novelist to undermine her own reputation by oversharing her personal life; when Anthony Trollope published his autobiography, he discussed money so relentlessly that he lost his audience for sixty or seventy years. But now the notorious Mitfords are fading into the past, and it is time for Nancy Mitford, the great novelist, to step forward.

Laughing to the End

George MacDonald Fraser would have you believe
that he died in 2008 an angry man. Or at least a disaf-
fected, curmudgeonly, irascible one. George MacDonald
Fraser, you will remember, wrote the Flashman series,
in which the nasty little bully of "Tom Brown's School
Days" (by Thomas Hughes) has grown up to be a cow-
ardly womanizer who just happens to save the day at
every miserable misadventure nineteenth-century British
forces engage in as they attempt to preserve the empire.

Fraser was a successful novelist, and he survived
himself by three days in order to damn the era of his
death in an article in the *Daily Mail*: "But much has
deteriorated. The United Kingdom has begun to look
more like a Third World country, shabby, littered, ugly,
run down, without purpose or direction, misruled by
a typical Third World government, corrupt, incom-
petent and undemocratic." In the *Weekly Standard*,
Christopher Hitchens quoted Fraser as saying of Tony
Blair, "It makes my blood boil to think of the British
soldiers who've died for that little liar." Blair haters
across the spectrum could sympathize. But a sad thing,
for me, is the way that Fraser's death was greeted by
organs of the right wing, such as the *Wall Street Journal*,
as another opportunity to bash liberals.

Anyone who has read the Flashman series will tell you that Flashy never saw an authoritarian or imperialist he couldn't make fun of—and cuckold too. In fact, the first person I knew who read and loved Flashy was a Marxist.

The Flashman books are purportedly drawn from a cache of papers detailing the exploits of Harry Flashman, who, after being expelled from the Rugby School, manages to get himself into the army just in time to be sent off to India. Flashy's virtues as a soldier are that he can ride a horse and wield a saber. His eye for a likely escape route is unexcelled. That he is a liar and a coward goes without saying, except by him. Flashy also has a wonderful sense of humor, which is his greatest charm. He particularly appreciates jokes of which he himself is the butt.

Once in India, Flashy is assigned to duty in the First Afghan War, and if the Soviets and Dick Cheney had bothered to read *Flashman* before they sent their troops in, we wouldn't be in the mess we got into in Afghanistan, and they wouldn't be in the mess they are in today. Fraser's historical research was meticulous and clearly presented, both in the text (because Flashy is a blowhard, always offering derisory opinions of the nonsensical aims of his superiors) and in the footnotes, which are written in their own skeptical style. The pointless difficulties of the First Afghan War are vividly demonstrated in *Flashman*, and in the course of the action many British soldiers do die for a lie.

Over his long career, Flashy gets to America (he's not in favor of slavery), to China, to Africa, to Russia. I have followed him happily on most of his adventures (though the passages about cricket in *Flashman's Lady* sank me). My second favorite, after *Flashman*, is *Flashman at the Charge*, about, among other things, the Crimean War. Fraser seems to have agreed with Charles Dickens that the level of incompetence the British manifested in the Crimea was unprecedented in its day. (To think we have surpassed it!) But, astonishingly, Fraser's analysis is both clearer and funnier than Dickens's.

One of the great things about Flashy is that even though he favors unprintable epithets for Blacks and Chinese and derogatory terms to describe nearly every type he meets (including women, Calvinists, and Scots), he's full of honest admiration for the decent and the brave, such as Abraham Lincoln, whom he encounters when Lincoln is a freshman congressman, in *Flash for Freedom!* Flashy is no right-winger; he's an anarchist and a populist, albeit a self-serving, lustful one. And that's another thing—he has honest admiration for female sexuality and power too.

If Fraser hadn't died, I would have loved to interview him at the Los Angeles Times Festival of Books. His career in Hollywood was as long as his career as the creator of the Flashman series (he also wrote several other books), and I thought it was a shame that he never appeared there. Perhaps he really was the dragon of his *Daily Mail* piece and would have burned me to a crisp right on the stage, but having read his latest novel—*The Reavers*, published in 2007—I think not. In fact, I think having a good laugh trumped all for George MacDonald Fraser.

Fraser was born just below the Scottish border (in Carlisle), and *The Reavers* is set in the Borders country (rather in the way *Cat Ballou* is set in the Old West) during the 1590s. The plot is long on action and short on sense, but Fraser's use of the English language is masterful and playful at the same time. My favorite character, a Scottish highwayman whose sex appeal is his deadliest weapon, speaks in carefully spelled-out dialect and is unfailingly funny. *The Reavers* is a novel-like confection that makes full use of the wealth of idioms, slang, and braggadocio (not omitting those current in Hollywood) that English has to offer. So, maybe Fraser's *Daily Mail* diatribe against political correctness was only his second-to-last word: maybe he died with a laugh on his lips, as I'm sure Harry Flashman did.

Farewell, Alice Munro, and Thanks for Everything

That Alice Munro titled her last volume of short stories *Dear Life* could not have been a surprise to her devoted readers. In even the most merciless stories in the fourteen volumes she has published since 1968, she has seemed steadily to embrace the energy of life itself. Fear and pain exist, but there is always something beyond the worst events—if not redemption or better times, then at least understanding or the outline of meaning. To me, this seems to be the quest of a writer who is above all curious, above all an investigator.

Munro once said of her ambitions: "What I wanted was every last thing, every layer of speech and thought, stroke of light on bark or walls, every smell, pothole, pain, crack, delusion, held still and held together—radiant, everlasting." When we read her work, we must be awed by that precision, by the way that her intent focus on the particular ends up illuminating the general. Munro is the only author whose writings are so vivid to me that I have occasionally mistaken incidents in her stories for memories of my own past.

Now, as of 2013, Munro is bowing out. She is eighty-two, and her husband died in April 2013; she is looking forward to doing something more sociable and less taxing than writing. Of course, I do not want to lose my access, as a reader, to her gaze upon the world, but I think it is a wise and telling choice. For one thing, she has, in the last four stories of *Dear Life*, revisited early material, rethought it in the wiser and more accepting terms that we would expect of someone who has spent most of her adult life maturing in the public eye. She has also recognized, perhaps, that every career has a natural arc and a natural end.

Not many successful writers have lived into their eighties—the perennially mature Henry James was seventy-two when he died, Tolstoy seventy-one when he published his last novel. Edith Wharton was working on *The Buccaneers* when she died at seventy-five. (Uncompleted, the novel was published the following year.) *The View from Castle Rock*, which Munro published when she was seventy-five, was a grand and intriguing departure, both geographically and thematically, and one of my favorites.

But now we must let her off the hook. Thank you, Alice Munro, for one glittering jewel of a story after another. Thank you for the many days and nights I spent lost in your work. Thank you for your unembarrassed woman's perspective on the lives of girls and women, but also the lives of boys and men. Thank you for your cruelty as well as your kindness, because the one plus the other is the essence of truthfulness.

History vs. Historical Fiction

In the late 1990s, when I first went blonde, I was driving to Santa Anita racetrack, and I turned in to the wrong entrance. I told a guard that I was looking for the main entrance, and he leaned forward and said in a loud, careful voice: "Okay. Go back out the way you came in, and then turn LEFT" (he demonstrated how to turn left by holding out his arms and making a left-turn gesture), "and then turn LEFT again [same gesture], and THAT'S the entrance." Big smile. I wondered for a moment why he was treating me like an idiot, and then I realized that I was now a blonde! Since I am very tall, always wear jeans, and can scowl with the best of them, being condescended to, even mansplained to, is something I have rarely endured, but it happened again this week, on BBC Radio 4's *Start the Week.* Only this time I was not condescended to as a blonde, I don't think, but as a novelist.

The condescender was Niall Ferguson, a conservative historian about fifteen years younger than I am, who wanted to be sure that I understood that the historical novel is all made up, but that historical nonfiction, written by historians, is truth. He referred to his research. I referred to my research. He wasn't convinced. I suggested that the demands of history and fiction are slightly different—that since a novel is a story, it must be complete, and since a history must be accepted by the reader as accurate, it must be incomplete. He was not convinced. He kept talking, I subsided, the program ended, but he did have the last word (apart from the host): he and the other historian agreed that the historical novel—even *War and Peace*—was a secondary form, at least compared with what they were doing.

I do not consider literary forms to exist in a hierarchy; I think of them as more of a flower bouquet, with different colors, scents, and shapes, each satisfying and unsatisfying in its way, but if there is one thing that I do know about history, it is that it must be based on the author's theory of what happened. He or she may change the theory as the research is completed, but without a theory, and if the research doesn't fit into the theory, then the text has no logic, and therefore makes no sense. If it makes no sense, then readers will not read it. A history book is, therefore, a construct. Because of archaeology, because of archives, because of historians, we live in an age where historical novels as a form are having a bit of a boom. Reading Pulitzer Prize–winning historical novelist Geraldine Brooks's list of her favorite historical novels in a magazine this week, I can only marvel at the variety of subject matter: Alexander the Great, the Lewis and Clark expedition, Ovid, the American Civil War. Of *Wolf Hall*, she writes: "Mantel seems to know Thomas Cromwell on the cellular level." I am sure that my historian-of-the-day would say that such a thing is impossible in a mere novel, but I would say that such a thing is possible only in a novel, because the job of a novelist is to do her (or his) best to see the world through her character's point of view—to imagine simultaneously what she and her subject are thinking and feeling as human beings, no matter how far apart they are, and also what is different about them—what has changed over the years and therefore indicates the passage of time and the change in the way people perceive things. This can be a challenge for a novelist, but it is also a pleasure, and the reason, after all, to write a historical novel.

Apart from my trilogy, The Last Hundred Years, I have written four historical novels: one set in medieval Greenland, one set in pre–Civil War Kansas, one set in Missouri and California between about 1885 and 1945, and one set in Monterey, California, in the early 1850s. Each presented different challenges, and of the four the third one, *Private Life*, was the hardest to write, simply because it was (at the time) the most recent—there was much more material to sift through and understand before I could cook it together and produce that fragrant stew we call a novel. *Private Life* is about a nice, normal midwestern woman who realizes that she has been married off to a crackpot and learns, for the most part, how to deal with him. My rule for myself as I wrote about the husband was that

I could think of him as a crackpot, but I could not diagnose him with any modern definitions—I wanted to see him as my female protagonist would see him, to feel the mystery of his unruly personality without putting him in any kind of a box. I used a somewhat archaic style to mimic how she might have thought of him and of the world she lived in. It took me a long time, and many drafts, but I believed in it in the end (that is, I was willing to suspend disbelief, and so were a fair number of readers). If my characters came alive and read my book, would they recognize themselves? I hope so. I did the research—into physics, into life in central Missouri and St. Louis, into the lasting effects of the Civil War, into the internment of the Japanese during World War II, into ferries running between San Francisco and Vallejo in the old days, into the history of Mare Island as a naval shipbuilding facility. (The buildings are still standing, as are the houses lived in by the officers stationed there by the US Navy.) As I looked at the houses when I was doing my research, I imagined my characters opening the blinds, dusting the furniture, chatting with their neighbors, making their way through days and weeks and years in that chilly, cloudy, but often beautiful climate. As a result of my fascination (and investigation), I certainly know more about that weird spot and its history than many historians do. My motto as a historical novelist has been: "You are there." But in order to put you there, I have to use my imagination to make connections, to evoke feelings, to show patterns, to build a logical structure. But then, my historian colleague must do the same. It is for the reader to decide which logical construct he or she believes.

Reflections on St. Louis

A couple of years ago, when I was looking into my family history, I discovered that after World War II, my grandfather, who worked at the International Shoe Company tannery over in Illinois, got a promotion, and he, my grandmother, and their two youngest kids moved to Bolivar, Tennessee. I looked up Bolivar on Google Maps and was not impressed. But they only lived in Bolivar for about two years. In the meantime, my mother, who had worked on the US Army newspaper during the war, returned, and went to work for the *Memphis Press-Scimitar.* And then, in the autumn of 1948, my parents, who had met during the war, got together, got married, and moved to LA, where my father was hoping to get a job at Hughes Aircraft. I was born in 1949. By late 1950, my parents' marriage was evidently not working out, and my mother had to bring me back to the Midwest. It was a scary time for my mother and my grandparents, but for me, it was the best possible piece of luck, because my grandfather had been transferred back to Hartford, and my grandparents bought a house in Webster Groves, on Clark Avenue.

Why was this my piece of luck, maybe the best piece of luck I've ever had? That is the theme of this essay.

I have very clear memories of Clark Avenue—of

our backyard, of Avery School and the walk to school, of the train tracks on Glen Road, of a friend's yard at Clark and Bompart that looked to me like a baseball field and is now just a sweet, green, triangular lawn. This is what happens after you grow up and move away—when you come back to visit, you see what things really look like, how they've changed, how you under- or overestimated what you were seeing when you were five or ten. But you also see how that environment made you, and what I see is how lucky I was to be situated in exactly that environment, Webster Groves, St. Louis County, up the street from Deer Creek, in one of the most historically interesting and complicated cities in the US, and, I would say, also one of the most beautiful and one of the most decrepit.

In October 2017, I brought my husband to St. Louis, where he had never been, since he grew up outside Philadelphia, for my fiftieth high school reunion. After the two or three days of reunion festivities, we stuck around to look around. We stayed at the Cheshire, rented a car, got out and about. My husband, who had been a realtor in Philly, was impressed and even amazed by the houses we drove past, and not only the new ones but the older ones, and not only the expensive ones but the eccentric less expensive ones. We also bantered back and forth about Cards fans vs. Phillies fans, how Phillies fans boo everything, but Cards fans always cheer. I took a walk in the foresty west area of Forest Park, and we went to the zoo, where I had gone often when I was growing up. I took out my phone, called my editor in the *New York Times* travel section, and said, "Have you ever thought about running a travel piece about St. Louis?" She said, "You're kidding me, right?" I said I would put together a draft and send it to her. It took her a long time to run it, because the travel section was backlogged, but they did run it, and that's why I'm giving this talk. Thank you for asking me. Since then, I've thought a lot more about what it has meant to me to grow up here, and every time, I am glad that I didn't grow up in LA, Memphis, or Bolivar.

Let's start with Webster Groves. My mother lived with my grandparents for a while while she worked in journalism. She was lucky to get hired by the *Globe-Democrat* as the Women's Page editor. This meant that we could move out, so first we moved to Cardinal Terrace, an apartment in Brentwood, and then to a small house on St. John Avenue, off Kirkham, in Webster. Every day, my mom dropped me off at Avery in the morning, and then I walked to my grandparents' house, always in the afternoon and sometimes for lunch. I loved walking, and as I got older, I expanded my area—first along Glen Road to Atalanta, or along Bompart to Atalanta, then down Marshall to the shopping area near Deer Creek Park, then around the Kirkham neighborhood, and then up into Old Orchard. The neighborhoods were small enough and close enough together that walking them was easy, even when I was ten or eleven. Maybe I was looking for candy, but I learned to look at the scenery—the creek, the trees, the houses. We had relatives in Webster Park and in the Central West End whom we would also visit, and my luck in this was that I saw all kinds of neighborhoods, all kinds of people, all kinds of flowers, trees, and vegetation. The effect that this had on me was that it made me curious.

At the time, though, the things I thought were pieces of good luck were the pony rides at the corner of Brentwood and Manchester, the movie theaters in Webster and on Brentwood down from the pony rides, the summer day camp not far from Grant's Farm (more horses), the Webster Groves public library, and then the St. Louis County public library. Horses and books were my two passions.

My mom had her own passions. One was fashion and one was meeting people, and she got to indulge both of those when she interviewed people such as Katherine Hepburn for the *Globe*, and when she got to put on her own fashion shows at Kiel Auditorium and also to go to New York for Fashion Week. Her passions affected mine, too, not because I shared them, but because they gave me the sense that in St. Louis, everything was possible—you could go any direction and explore anything. What also gave me this feeling was my grandfather's habit of singing "Oh, Shenandoah," as we crossed the wide Missouri. I knew our family had come from Norway, Minnesota, Idaho, and Virginia. Ending up in St. Louis was a piece of luck, because not only could you think about the nation that spread out around us but you could get there by road, by train, by plane.

Just before I turned eleven, my mother remarried. My stepfather, a wonderful man, personified another part of St. Louis. He was Catholic, he had grown up around Carondolet, had gone to St. Louis University High. After working at Price Waterhouse as an accountant, he ended up as president of Petrolite. We knew about Petrolite because my grandparents' house in Webster was half a mile up the road from a company Petrolite owned, Tretolite, an oil pipe plant—when there was an explosion there sometime when I was a baby, I was napping; my mother ran outside to catch me if I flew out the window, and my Aunt Nancy went to my crib, picked me up, and carried me outside. What I didn't know about was Creve Coeur, Ladue. My new stepsister went to Villa Duchesne, my new stepbrother went to Chaminade, our church was Ste. Genevieve du Bois. I might as well have moved to France. As for sophistication, my parents ate out every Sunday, all over town, sometimes at the Missouri Athletic Club, which gave me a chance to see the varied and intriguing buildings along Locust or Washington.

My mother's dream for me came true—I went first to Community School, then to John Burroughs. My world opened up like a book, because of books.

Where I live now, in Carmel Valley, California, it is sixteen and a half miles to the most historic building on the peninsula, Colton Hall. On the way, I see many beautiful hills, mountains, and trees, some lovely houses, and two shopping malls, and I also get glimpses of the ocean. If I were to drive eighteen miles in St. Louis, I could get from Wood Acre, where our house was after my mother remarried, to my grandparents' house on Clark, to 19 Dartford, where my mother lived after Wood Acre, just west of Forest Park, and then to the Arch. On the way, I would see a vast array of different landscapes and cityscapes—houses that are so elegant that they defy belief; houses that are empty, with their roofs collapsed; houses that are modest but appealing in green and pleasant yards; many parks; a few junkyards, elegant shops, and restaurants; Busch Stadium; as well as a variety of neighborhoods and citizens that would be, in and of themselves, a lesson in the history of St. Louis and, you might say, the entire US.

When I was sixteen and had my driver's license, that trip was not my choice. What I preferred was driving into the countryside—Chesterfield, across the river, sometimes as far as Wildwood. I looked for horses, gazing at the countryside and the hills, the trees blooming in the spring and turning in the fall. St. Louis is a spot where everything is available—urbanity and natural beauty, elegance and culture, but also conflict, decay, violence, and pollution. It is therefore a perfect spot for a future novelist to grow up.

A few years ago, I did a review for the *New World Review* of Walter Johnson's detailed history of St. Louis, *The Broken Heart of America*. Johnson is a professor at

Harvard and grew up in Columbia, where his father taught at Mizzou. As familiar as I thought I was with the history of St. Louis, most of what Johnson discussed was new to me. It is a long and fascinating book, and my first response was to cry, and even argue. My experiences here as a child did not make me think that St. Louis was racist—Avery School desegregated without a problem; I never heard the N-word in the house, or even on the street. An African American couple lived down the street in Webster, and we had fun with their grandchildren when they came for a visit. We admired Bob Gibson, we listened to Chuck Berry and Tina Turner. But Johnson's book is not about our individual feelings and perceptions; it is about how St. Louis was used, by the North and the South, as the jumping-off place for the conquest of America and the establishment of capitalist white dominance across the continent. Why didn't I know that? No one, no teacher or parent said a word about it. Among the many unjust and disheartening details, the one that somehow struck me the most was about the Dred Scott decision. I never knew, and we were never told in American History class, about a lesser-known legal decision that preceded it: A woman slave, Winny, was taken by her owner from Illinois to St. Louis in 1818. She sued for her freedom and won her case in 1824 on the grounds that she had lived for several years in free territory. Subsequently, several hundred slaves won their freedom in Missouri using her case as precedent. The Dred Scott case was a reaction to thirty years of enslaved African Americans' successfully using legal means to fight slavery. All through his history, Johnson details the back-and-forth nature of St. Louis: the setbacks, such as the Dred Scott decision, followed by the progress—for example, "By the time the Missouri State Constitution of 1865 made their legal emancipation official and irrevocable, most of those who had been enslaved in St. Louis had long since claimed freedom for themselves. Three public schools for African American children were opened in 1866, and in 1868, public street cars became legally integrated."

I more or less left St. Louis when I went to college in 1967. My habit of looking around stuck with me. I was fascinated by upstate New York and impressed by New York City. I traveled through Europe for a year after college, then ended up in Iowa, where I studied at the University of Iowa for six years and taught at Iowa State for sixteen years. But I owe my literary career to my education at John Burroughs, where we read lots and lots of wonderful books and plays, by Dickens, Hawthorne, Shakespeare, Ole Rolvaag, and many others, and I owe *A Thousand Acres* not only to Shakespeare but also to Barry Commoner, who taught at Wash U for thirty-four years. I had just moved to Iowa, and I was living in an old farmhouse thirty miles outside town. I picked up *The Closing Circle*, and chapter 5 was about nitrogen fertilizer, nitrates in wells, and the conversion of nitrates into poisonous nitrites in the human body. We were drinking from a well, living among farmers.

I never forgot it. Fifteen years later, when I was driving with my husband through the flats of north central Iowa and reading about miscarriages and diseases that grew out of the fact that the farm fields returned the pesticides and fertilizers directly to the wells, thereby causing a spike in all kinds of health problems, I said, "This is where I am going to set that Lear novel." That husband, who was from Clinton, Iowa, and learned to swim across the Mississippi when he was about fourteen, was hot to get out of the Midwest, so we moved to California, where I still live.

Because of my relatives who still lived in St. Louis, I did come back often, sometimes for Christmas, sometimes in the summer, but I was focused on visiting the relatives, not on looking around. One place that really struck me, though, in 2016, was the senior living facility that my aunt, then eighty-nine, could afford in Webster. It was a former convent. The building was striking, but the rooms were small, and her bathroom was down a long hallway. Fortunately, she was about as active as an eighty-nine-year-old could be, so that didn't bother her. I was of two minds about her place—it was way more interesting than my mother's facility in Palo Alto, but it also demonstrated the downside of repurposing older buildings and not being able to update them.

The reason I was invited to write this essay, for a talk, was the publication of my *NYT* travel piece. When I saw it in print, the thing I loved was the photographs Whitney Curtis took—a view of downtown from the bridge at the

City Museum, a wall of flowers at the Botanical Garden, elephants and branches of leaves at the zoo, the interior of the Sugarfire Barbecue restaurant. The photos expressed my pleasure in my visit to St. Louis, but they didn't express my doubts. The article was long, and it got 352 comments—the article touched a chord, but it was not always a harmonious chord. Some readers were pleased with the article, and some extremely displeased, because they were annoyed that I hadn't sufficiently discussed violence, racism, and economic disparity in St. Louis. (But, I might have said in response to "Mark," this is a travel article—do travel articles about Marseille and Rome offer those observations to tourists?) My two favorite comments were by Zelda Beckowitz, who wrote, "Jane Smiley has provided a well-written and comprehensive piece, but I must agree with other commenters that she overlooked the spectre of danger that haunts the city," and Charles Michener, who wrote, "I wish Jane Smiley had mentioned that St. Louis is a major mecca for lovers of 20th century art. . . . Not bad for a place that 'most Americans [don't] view as a tourist destination.'"

These days, when I read my digital *Post Dispatch*, I am saddened by the murder rate, which is on track to be the highest ever; the stubborn COVID rate; and the fact that the Cards lost more games than the Cubs this weird season. But nothing I read in the *Post* makes St. Louis an outlier—COVID and chaos are everywhere. Two of my children live in COVID hotspots, New York and LA; my son and daughter-in-law live in

Northern California, and her parents have been living with them because they had to escape a fire in which several of their friends lost their homes. We had to escape our own fire a month ago. I wonder whether the thirteenth-century inhabitants of the Cahokia Mounds, who had to leave the spot they built because of climate change and overuse of the local resources, are gazing down at us from somewhere and saying, "We told you so." The last chapter of Walter Johnson's book discusses the resilience of St. Louis—individuals and organizations in town that are working hard to develop a more sustainable and equitable society—and he also makes sure we know that this isn't a new thing; it has been going on as long as there has been a St. Louis. I hope it works; I hope it spreads up and down the Mississippi, out along the Ohio and the Missouri. It could end up that the future that is imagined in St. Louis really is our future as a country. And I hope that it re-creates the pleasures of the city that are what I see when I think of my childhood memories, memories of strange and beautiful houses and neighborhoods jammed up against one another; of green parks and lovely vistas; of a long history of interesting and accomplished citizens; of great places to visit, such as the art museum, Circus Harmony, the Botanical Garden, and Forest Park; of friendly people and good teachers. No matter what I've learned and what the critics say, I can't get rid of those memories. All I can do is hope that future generations will have the chance to enjoy similar ones.

Writing Is an Exercise in Freedom

I read **Oliver Twist** in seventh grade and *Great Expectations* in eighth, and I hated them both. So when I was assigned *David Copperfield* in ninth grade, I put it off for as long as I could. Finally, of course, a deadline forced me to get started. I went down to the basement and read the entire thing in one weekend. And it caught me off guard—I adored it. This was where my love of Dickens started.

When I got to college, I didn't read any Dickens. I was an English major, but I focused mostly on medieval stuff. I don't know why I picked up *Our Mutual Friend* during my senior year, over Christmas vacation. But I remember how I sat out by the Christmas tree, just reading and reading, completely absorbed by it.

Of all of the Dickens I've read, including everything I studied for the biography I wrote, *Our Mutual Friend* remains my favorite. There are so many interesting things about the book. First of all, it has one of the greatest portraits of a stalker you could ever imagine. And Dickens plays with the novel's conventions in fascinating ways. The standard romance ends with the happily married couple, for instance—but here

Dickens moves beyond the wedding into the marriage itself, exploring how a successful love story works itself out with time. By this stage of his career, Dickens was old and very famous; he knew he could do whatever he wanted. You can see him playing with established elements of the genre, subverting them, and it's part of this novel's greatness to me.

But there was a more immediate, straightforward connection—I simply loved his descriptions. Although I had read lots of books before *Our Mutual Friend*, this was the one that made me think: I've got to do this. I've got to try to write novels. It's just too interesting to pass up—I can't go on and be a lawyer now. (Not that I ever wanted to be a lawyer, but I might have gone on to be a vet or something.) After *Our Mutual Friend*, other careers were no longer an option. I had to try this novel-writing thing, because the images Dickens uses are so great and riveting.

Dickens's descriptive powers are on display throughout *Our Mutual Friend*, but one of my favorite examples concerns the bad guys. Not the really bad guys, but the sort-of-bad guys—Mr. and Mrs. Lammle, two small-time swindlers who marry each other for money. On their honeymoon, they each find out that the other person has pretended to be wealthy, so they're forced to go on swindling other people together.

Mr. Lammle is sort of a villain, but he's enjoyably villainous. In the last section of the novel, Dickens describes him in a way I love:

Up came the sun, steaming all over London, and
in its glorious impartiality even condescending
to make prismatic sparkles in the whiskers of
Mr Alfred Lammle as he sat at breakfast.

I've always remembered the image of Lammle's
beard sparkling in the sunlight. I can see the little
breakfast nook. I can see him sitting at the table. I can
see his beard, and I can see the sunlight sparkling in
his beard. We already know by this time that Lammle
is extremely mercenary, so Dickens is highlighting the
impartiality of the sunlight—the way it can beautify
anything, good or bad. We know Lammle's a scammer,
but there's this beautiful moment anyway. And there's
a kind of magical foreshadowing at work, too: the way
the sun shines down, making his beard sparkle, signals
that something unusual is coming, some unusual plot
twist—as indeed it does come.

As a reader, and as a writer, I love images and
sentences that are so striking that you remember and
cherish them. Because they're embedded in a huge
amount of language, such standout lines and descriptions must truly be extraordinary. *Our Mutual Friend* is
probably a two-hundred-thousand-word novel; there
are probably ten thousand sentences. Yet as the reader
goes along reading this abundance of sentences, from
time to time one grabs and holds on. To me, that's
the essence of the novel: the tension between wanting to linger in appreciation of an individual line and

wanting to see what happens next. You must move on, if you're ever going to finish the book—especially one as long as *Our Mutual Friend*—and yet certain details capture you, slow you, ask you to pause. It's because of this experience that I love novels most among the art forms. When you're reading a poem, you're asked to linger. If a poem is one hundred words long, you're asked to pay attention to each word. But when you're reading a novel, you're asked to keep moving—yet you resist this forward motion when certain lines demand your attention.

The moments are what come to mind when I think about the books I like best—moments that stick in my mind as pictures. When you're deep into reading a book that you're very fond of, the images pass through your mind and leave a permanent impression. I don't tend to remember the ideas as strongly. For me, a novel's conceptual framework generally takes a backseat to the images that tell the story. Ultimately, these images are more important and enduring than what the writer believes.

There are novelists I love who have advanced their theories about how the world works, how life works, and so on. One of my favorite examples is Émile Zola. But though the theories may motivate the novel, and they may help structure the novel, they fall by the wayside almost always. The enduring things are the story, the characters, the scenes.

The reader has to have images in order to feel

oriented in the world of the novel. We must be able to see our way around. Your images may not be the same as my images—different readers will perceive a novel's world differently, depending on what they notice and respond to in the descriptions—but the visual details are our entry into the story.

It's fascinating that readers can have images of places they have never seen. Recently, I met someone who grew up in Russia. One of her favorite books had been *Huckleberry Finn*, while one of my favorite books was Dostoevsky's novel *Crime and Punishment*. There's a scene in *Crime and Punishment* where a horse and carriage are going down the road, and the driver whips the horse so badly that it falls to its knees in the street and dies. I remember being fifteen and reading that, and imagining that I could see all St. Petersburg, and within it that horse dying in the middle of the street. Simultaneously there was somebody in Russia imagining Huckleberry Finn going down an American river she had never seen. I believed in my images, and she believed in hers. These mental images—created in collaboration with the author—are what give one's love of a story a base.

Dickens was extremely observant. People who knew him or met him were sometimes taken aback by how he seemed to be scanning them. He was observant not just visually, but aurally—he was a practiced eavesdropper. Many moments that the rest of us might pass over, he would note, and they would filter into his work.

I think he created his images both consciously and unconsciously, as all novelists do. By the time writers are as old and practiced as Dickens was, the choice of imagistic details is not really a conscious thing. As you sit there, starting a new chapter, your mind goes *hmmm*—and then, bingo. It's on the page. It's not as though you've sorted through every image in your brain and picked the best one. It's more that you knew what the theme of the chapter was going to be, and this thought or image cropped up as one way in. It gave you energy, and off you went.

Often the story details we choose have an unconscious, unintended power. For example, in *Our Mutual Friend*, the stalker is a young man who's a teacher, born poor, uneasy about his social mobility. During the day, he attempts to do a good job with his teaching—but during the night, he stalks the gentleman Eugene Wrayburn. It's this social uneasiness that makes him more and more aggressive as he stalks his aristocratic target. I don't think we can read *Our Mutual Friend* without seeing this stalker as a kind of weird self-portrait of Dickens and his social rise. But it's very possible Dickens didn't intend this at all. Maybe he just drew upon his own life—his experiences as a kind of social weirdo in the class system of England—in order to portray a stalker's obsessiveness.

This unconscious power is often tapped through the act of description, and unexpected story revelations can spring out of the physical details of a scene.

The images themselves, in other words, can contain clues about where the story needs to go. When I was first starting my novel *Moo*, for instance, I was describing some abandoned buildings that my character Chairman X was looking at. Suddenly, he saw a young man going inside, though he didn't know why anyone would enter an abandoned building. Well, I didn't know why either! But this man went in, even though I had never thought about those buildings or that man before. Suddenly, I had to find out what was inside. As it turned out, the giant pig Earl Butz—the hog at the center of the finished novel—was inside. Earl Butz hadn't been part of the plan before that point. But as the book progressed, the secret I discovered in those buildings became essential to the novel.

That kind of experience is what I always want: the energy that comes from sudden inspiration. That's what inspiration is to me—the idea that gives unexpected energy to the narrative. Work that is too planned out often doesn't have that kind of energy.

That's why you cannot be judging yourself as you write the first draft—you want to harness that unexpected energy, and you don't want to limit the possibilities of exploration. You don't know what you're writing until it's done. So if a draft is five hundred pages long, you have to suspend judgment for months. It takes effort to be good at suspending judgment, to give the images and story priority over your ideas. But you keep going, casting about for the next sentence. I think there are two kinds of sentences in a rough draft: seeds and pebbles. If it's a pebble, it's just the next sentence and it sits there. But if it's a seed, it grows into something that becomes an important part of the life of the novel. The problem is, you can't know ahead of time whether a sentence will be a seed or a pebble, or how important a seed it's going to be. That bit of *Moo* turned out to be an important seed. But if Chairman X had turned away and had another thought—had I stuck with my plan and insisted the man entering the buildings was just a pebble—the book might have gone in a different direction.

This is why it's important to remain open to the unexpected. The writing experience is in some ways like riding a bucking bronco—sometimes he's good and sometimes he bucks you off, sometimes he follows orders, sometimes he spooks. I like that unexpected quality. You have to be able to keep riding whatever comes.

Of course, I don't want to suggest that one's ideas and beliefs have no place in the novel. They're important. One's ideas can inspire the story. The writing process is an interplay between the ideas you begin with and the story that emerges despite what you think. The story and the ideas talk back and forth to one another. As I write, my ideas about the book may inform how the characters think, how the story works itself out, what happens. But at a certain point, the characters start to take on their own life—and they begin to transcend the ideas that initially inspired them.

For example: in volume 3 of the trilogy I published in 2014 and 2015, there's a good guy and a bad guy. I thought of them as "good" and "bad." But when I went back for the last rewrite, I was surprised by how appealing the bad guy was. The idea part of me thought, "Well, maybe I need to make him more of a scumbag." But the novelist part of me said, "No. Ambiguity is always good."

So you learn to expect the unexpected, and make allowances for it. There's a constant back-and-forth between what you planned and what you didn't plan, and how you are going to reconcile the two. I guess that's what drafts are for—negotiating how much plan to preserve, how much newness to let in.

I think all novel writing, and all art, is a form of play—and it's the unexpected that gives it the playful aspect, while ideas give it the serious aspect. When the unexpected crops up, that's like playing a game where your body has to catch the ball you didn't even realize a moment ago was heading in your direction. I like this aspect of play; I think it's wonderful—and makes it all worth doing.

When I was a student at the Iowa Writers' Workshop, I remember opening the door to my friend's office and looking inside. Over her desk, above her typewriter, she'd tacked up a phrase: NOBODY ASKED YOU TO WRITE THAT NOVEL. I knew right away this was going to be an important idea for me. The line reminded me that writing was a voluntary activity.

I could always stop. I could always go on. And since no one's asking me to do it, I've always seen writing as an exercise of freedom, rather than an exercise of obligation. Even when it came to be that writing was my income, it still seemed like an exercise of freedom. Yes, writing is my job—but I could always stop and do something else. Once writing becomes an exercise of freedom, it's filled with energy.

I remember when I proposed *A Thousand Acres* to my agent, she said, "Are you kidding me? No one wants to read a novel about farming." But no one was going to stop me. "We'll see," I said, and I just wrote it. That's been the case for all my books, successful or not successful. I wrote the books I wanted to write. I know I've been lucky to be able to write this way.

To me as a reader, the greatest thing about the novel—I start sentences this way all the time, but I always say a different thing—is that it gives access to the mind of the writer. *Our Mutual Friend* is a perfect example of this: you have access to the mind of this guy, Charles Dickens. Prolonged access, 880 pages of access. There is no intermediary between you and this guy's mind. There are no actors, no stage production. To read a book is an act of humanity. It's an act of connection. And it's also an act of freedom— at any point, I could say, I'm done with *Our Mutual Friend*, I'm moving on to Anthony Trollope. As long as you're reading, you're there voluntarily. To me, that's the essence of the novel: accessing the mind of

another human being in a way that combines freedom with intimacy. This is a rare thing. You don't get
it through an interview; you don't get it through relationships—other people can always withhold information from you. You don't get this kind of access in
any other art—poetry, maybe, but the contact isn't as
prolonged. I find it perennially alluring. I've been at
this for years, yet this voluntary act of connection still
fascinates me in my reading and my writing.

About the Author

Jane Smiley is a novelist and essayist. Her novel *A Thousand Acres* won the Pulitzer Prize and the National Book Critics Circle Award in 1992, and her novel *The All-True Travels and Adventures of Lidie Newton* won the 1999 Spur Award for Best Novel of the West. She has been a member of the American Academy of Arts and Letters since 1987. Her novel *Horse Heaven* was short-listed for the Orange Prize in 2002, and her novel *Some Luck* was long-listed for the 2014 National Book Award. She has written for numerous magazines and newspapers, including the *New Yorker*, the *New York Times*, *Harper's*, and the *Nation*. Her most recent novel, *A Dangerous Business*, was published in 2022. She lives in Carmel Valley, California.

A Note on Type

The Questions That Matter Most is set primarily in Baskerville, one of the preeminent typefaces in book publishing. Designed by John Baskerville in the eighteenth century, and building on the innovations of William Caslon, the typeface broke ground particularly in the aesthetic unity of its roman and italic characters. John Baskerville cared especially about making high-quality books that would last, and his dedication has borne out in the legacy of his namesake typeface, which has remained a standard well into the digital age, with contemporary designers continuing to refine and experiment with it.

For numerals this book employs Minion Pro, an Adobe Original typeface designed by Robert Slimbach and first presented in 1990. The display text is set in Eloquent JF Pro, designed by Jason Walcott at Adobe Fonts; it is a revival of Pistilli Roman, which was created by Herb Lubalin and John Pistilli and released in 1964.

The cover for this edition of *The Questions That Matter Most* features two fonts in addition to the handwritten title text. The subtitle, as well as the line below Jane Smiley's name, uses Frontage Condensed, designed and published by Juri Zaech. Jane Smiley's name is set in Leviathan Black, which was designed by Jonathan Hoefler and Tobias Frere-Jones and published by Hoefler & Co.